A GUIDE TO THE PLANT HEALTH CARE MANAGEMENT SYSTEM
— SECOND EDITION —

AUTHORS

M. A. L. SMITH, A. G. ENDRESS,
G. R. SMITH, AND J. E. LLOYD
UNIVERSITY OF ILLINOIS

R. D. NEELY
ILLINOIS NATURAL HISTORY SURVEY

R. K. STUTMAN
COMMUNICATION RESEARCH ASSOCIATES

J. J. BALL
SOUTH DAKOTA STATE UNIVERSITY

K. D. CODER
THE UNIVERSITY OF GEORGIA

T. L. WADLEY
KELLY & ASSOCIATES

T. L. WADLEY, EDITOR

Development of the Plant Health Care
Management System was originally funded in part by:
USDA Forest Service
International Society of Arboriculture Research Trust
National Arborist Foundation

An official publication of
International Society of Arboriculture

Book design and production by
Kelly & Associates, Homer, Illinois

Printed by Kowa Graphics, Champaign, Illinois

Copyright © 1995 by International Society of Arboriculture.
All rights reserved. Printed in the United States of America.

Except as permitted under the United States Copyright Act of 1976, no part of this publication may be reproduced or distributed in any form or by any means, or stored in a data base or retrieval system, without prior written permission of the International Society of Arboriculture.

ISBN 1-881956-09-1

10 9 8 7 6 5 4 3 2 1

International Society of Arboriculture
P.O. Box GG
Savoy, IL 61874-9902 USA
Phone 217-355-9411

Introduction

For centuries people have both enjoyed and used the trees that grace much of our landscape. Today, for the millions of people living in urban and suburban centers, trees in their community forests have become particularly important. The public is increasingly aware of the environmental and ecological importance of trees and the significant societal benefits that can be gained from trees in the landscape. This is readily confirmed by the momentum and enthusiasm of a myriad of global tree planting movements.

Trees are an important element and symbol relating to human activities and environmental quality. This is particularly true for individuals living in developed urban areas. It is here that trees are few in number and are viewed as a resource that contributes in many meaningful ways to a pleasant and wholesome environment and to the quality of life.

While the public views trees as positive elements in their lives, most people are also increasingly concerned about the declining overall quality of the environment. They are concerned about air pollution, water quality, energy usage, climate change, and the use of chemicals in the landscape. All of these concerns revolve around the central thread of negative human behavior and the environmental consequences that result from it.

Urban forests are comprised of the many thousands of trees along streets and in parks, residential yards and gardens, and other open spaces. Urban forests that can help soak up pollution, capture and store carbon dioxide, and literally air condition the urban environment. These living forests support a wide variety of other plants and wildlife, bring cohesion to the urban design, enhance and reinforce the surrounding architecture, and sustain the human spirit through the recreation, aesthetic, and psychological values they provide.

Commercial and municipal arborists have a difficult task in caring for trees in urban environments. Urban surroundings, with often compacted soils, air pollution, elevated temperatures, and inadequate growing areas are harsh for trees. All too often tree care professionals have been forced to exercise crisis management, dealing with stress-laden and pest-infested trees because inadequate attention was given to site and tree selection, and post-planting care and maintenance.

Managing the health of trees has never been easy. There are thousands of tree species and cultivars. Each has its own climate and cultural requirements for best growth and each is prone to a variety of pests. With the beginning of the chemical age, agriculturists and arborists used pesticides, the new chemical weapons, to combat the many pests of our crop and landscape plants. Sometimes these chemicals were used with little discretion. And sometimes these chemicals were properly used given the knowledge at the time, but new research results later showed long-term detrimental impacts.

Not all insects are harmful — in fact, only a few are pests. New chemical weapons had been developed that targeted these specific pests. Although the weapons became more sophisticated, our treatment strategies remained the same. We fell into the rut of constantly reacting to the presence of pests by even more treatments, sometimes compounding our problems.

Today we can break this reactive treatment cycle. Today we have effective alternatives for the control of insects and diseases. Today, through ongoing research, we have a much better understanding of the systems of living things interacting in the landscape. Today we have the capacity to facilitate natural processes rather than disrupt or destroy them. Today we have an effective and responsible technology for managing plant health. Today we have a solution with both human and plant benefits.

The solution is Plant Health Care (PHC), a stunningly simple and elegant, yet multifaceted and comprehensive concept in plant management. It is a concept with which arborists and plant owners can grow and thrive.

About this Book

This book is designed to provide landscape care companies with information essential to implementing a Plant Health Care (PHC) practice. Care has been taken to be thorough and to present material in a way that facilitates readability. All employees, regardless of their function within the company, should be encouraged to read this book to gain an understanding of the various aspects of the Plant Health Care Management System. Important PHC terms are highlighted throughout the book in ***bold italics***.

The depth of this program becomes evident when viewing the Table of Contents on the following pages. Chapter One provides a thorough overview of the Plant Health Care concept. Chapters two through six address various aspects of PHC marketing. Chapter Two provides insight into plant care consumer beliefs, attitudes, behaviors and desires. Chapter Three provides general business considerations and Chapter Four walks you through the creation of your own marketing plan. Chapter Five offers information and tips for creatively selling PHC services. Chapter six provides information on the all-important issue of pricing for profitability.

A summary of the technical information supporting the Plant Health Care Management System comprises chapters seven through eleven — providing implementation details to make PHC work for you. Monitoring, site inventories, diagnosis, technical resources, pest control, stress management, record keeping, follow-up evaluations, and customer information and communication are the cornerstones supporting the PHC approach. Separate sections provide information about each of these essential PHC components.

Chapter Twelve focuses on PHC benefits and implementation details for landscape design/build professionals.

Table of Contents

CHAPTER ONE
Plant Health Care (PHC): An Overview / 1

Introduction	1
PHC and the HMO: An Analogy	1
PHC Is a Contractual Service	3
PHC: A Natural Integration	4
Regular On-site Visits — A PHC Imperative	4
The Evolution of PHC	5
Key Plant Concept	6
Key Stress Concept	6
Chapter Summary	7

CHAPTER TWO
PHC Marketing: The Consumers / 9

Introduction	9
Who Are Tree Care Consumers?	9
Tree Care Consumers Are Not Environmentalists	10
Tree Care Consumers Desire Information	11
Consumers Have Low Expectations Regarding Tree Care Services	11
Mystery of Consumer Desires	13
Mystery Study #1: Deborah and Sam	13
Mystery Study #2: Susan	14
Mystery Study #3: Diane and Bill	14
Consumer Profiles	15
Moving Forward	16
Chapter Summary	17

CHAPTER THREE
PHC Marketing: Strategies and Planning / 19

Introduction	19
From the Present to the Future	19
General Marketing Review	21
Your Marketing Mission	22
An Objective Look at Subjective Issues	23
Chapter Summary	23

CHAPTER FOUR
The PHC Marketing Plan / 25

Introduction	25
Examining Your Marketing Culture	25
Choosing a Marketing Theme	27
Developing a Theme Focus	28
Branding Your PHC Service	29
Market Segmentation	29
Target Marketing	30
The Competition	30
Marketing Objectives	31
Sales Objectives	31
Marketing Mix	31
Advertising	32
Other Promotional Activities	34
Publicity	34
Production	35
The PHC Marketing Plan	35
Chapter Summary	37

CHAPTER FIVE
PHC Marketing: Selling the Service / 39

Introduction	39
Customized Promotional Materials	39
Information Brochure Promotion	39
Tree Valuation Promotion	40
Developing a PHC Sales Path	40
PHC Video, Sales Aids and Compendium	48
Chapter Summary	48

CHAPTER SIX
PHC Marketing: Pricing Programs / 51

Introduction	51
Tree Management Approach	51
Example of Tree Management Pricing	52
Landscape Management Approach	52
Inventories	52

Maintenance Contract 53
　　　Monitoring 54
　　　Pesticide Treatments 54
　　　Monitoring Reports 55
　　　Fertilizing 55
　　　Pruning 55
　　　Shearing 55
　　　Example of Landscape Management Pricing 56
Chapter Summary 57

CHAPTER SEVEN
PHC Monitoring and Inventory / 59

Introduction 59
Monitoring 59
Scheduled Monitoring 60
Public or Client Relations 61
Routine Monitoring 61
Materials Needed for Monitoring 64
Background Education or Training 65
Inventory the Site 65
Identify the Landscape Plants 65
　　　Importance of Accurate Plant Identification 65
　　　Features Used in Woody Plant Identification 66
Identify Key Plants, Key Stresses 70
Developing Strategies 73
Record Site Specifics 73
　　　Site Factors: Climate 74
　　　Site Factors: Soil 76
　　　Site Factors: Injury and Stress 76
　　　Site Factors: Maintenance 78
Preparing a Landscape Map 79
Chapter Summary 82

CHAPTER EIGHT
PHC Diagnosis / 85

Introduction 85
Diagnosis of Plant Diseases and Insect Problems 86
Tools for Diagnosis and Their Uses 87
　　　Essential Tools 87
　　　Special Function Tools 88
Siting, Selecting, and Planting Problems 89
Problems Arising from Maintenance 91
Diseases 92
　　　Leaf Diseases on Deciduous Trees 92
　　　Leaf Diseases on Deciduous Conifers 93
　　　Leaf and Twig Diseases 94

Stem and Root Diseases	94
Systemic Diseases	95
Insects	95
Sucking Insects	97
Chewing Insects	97
Mining Insects	98
Boring Insects	98
Gall Forming Insects	99
Mites	99
Chapter Summary	99

CHAPTER NINE
Technical Resources and Strategies / 101

Introduction	101
Extension Agents/University Researchers/Specialists	101
Facilitated Library Searches	102
Suggested Key References for Specific Topics	102
On the Overall PHC Concept	102
On Woody Plant Identification	102
On Key Plants/Key Stress	102
On Site Inventory and Importance of Site Factors to Tree Health	102
On Establishing a Map and the Value of Individual Landscape Plants	103
Internet Electronic Information Resource	103
Professional Experience	103
PHC Strategies	104
Management Strategies	105
Prevention/Avoidance	105
Management	107
Management Options	110
Cultural	110
Biological	110
Chemical	113
Combined Tactics	114
Chapter Summary	116

CHAPTER TEN
Record Keeping and Evaluation / 117

Introduction	117
Treatment Records	118
Regulatory Requirements	119
Additional Records	120
Follow-up/Evaluation	120
Accuracy of Diagnosis/Effectiveness of Treatment	120
Cost Effectiveness	123

Schedule for Future Action 124
Client Information and Communication 125
Contracts/Proposals 125
Reports 127
Notices/Inserts 129
Billings/Service Evaluations 130
Guarantees 130
Chapter Summary 131

CHAPTER ELEVEN
PHC Equipment and Staffing / 133

Introduction 133
Upgrade of Equipment and Staff 133
Equipment 134
    Vehicles 134
    Spray Equipment 134
Staffing 135
Program Expansion 135
Chapter Summary 139

CHAPTER TWELVE
PHC and the Landscape Design/Build Process / 141

Introduction 141
Incorporating PHC into the Design Process 142
Marketing PHC Landscapes 144
Monitoring Needs of a New Landscape 147
PHC Beyond the First Year 148
Chapter Summary 148

CHAPTER

Plant Health Care (PHC): An Overview

INTRODUCTION

PHC is a multi-dimensional strategy for plant care which reaches beyond traditional techniques.

Trees are valuable long-term assets that deserve and require long-term care. As the professionals who care about and for trees, arborists must be committed to providing services that preserve the vitality — safety, health, and appearance — of the urban and community forest. Since urban environments are shared by both plants and humans, plant care must be safe, environmentally-sensitive, and cost-effective. These are the fundamental goals and benefits of the *Plant Health Care Management System (PHC)*.

PHC is a powerful, multi-dimensional management strategy for plant care which reaches beyond traditional techniques. This approach focuses on plant vitality and relies on selection and integration of a broad range of techniques aimed at protecting and enhancing plant health. PHC additionally focuses on the client who expects personalized attention, information, and beautiful and effective plants.

On the surface PHC appears to be complex because of its many facets (Figure 1-1). However, once a thorough overview is gained, the big picture reveals a fairly simple new approach to doing business in the tree care industry. It is indeed a departure from traditional methods of landscape care. PHC requires changes in thinking and attitudes. The arborist must assume a proactive position which emphasizes the health of plants rather than a reactive response to symptoms of problems. Properly implemented, a PHC program can produce substantial profits, provide cost-effective services to clients, instill client confidence and loyalty, and create an image of professionalism.

This chapter is designed to provide an overview. Much of the information presented here will be amplified in later chapters. Let's get started by comparing the Plant Health Care Management System to another familiar concept.

PHC AND THE HMO: AN ANALOGY

HMOs (Health Maintenance Organizations) have become popular in human health management in recent years. If not members of such an organization, we are all at least familiar with the concept. Typically, a member must sign a contract and make periodic payments. For doing this, a person can expect personalized attention from a caring, responsive and professional staff with an interest in maintaining his/her health. In order to put the goals of PHC in perspective, we can draw an analogy with these familiar principles.

Not long ago, people were very willing to "take some medicine" whenever they became ill. Now the general public is more wary of potential hazards of many drugs (in the same way that the public is more cognizant of potential hazards with overused and improper chemical applications). People are now aware, thanks to education and the popular press, that there are many components to health maintenance, including proper diet, exercise, and management of stress. Among approaches to good health, prevention now occupies the front seat, ahead of treatment or therapy.

Both PHC and human health maintenance use holistic approaches to establish and sustain health. Simple principles are the foundation of these approaches:

- preventive care for stress management;
- frequent monitoring;
- early detection of problems;
- informed decision making;
- integrated treatments to provide long-term,stable solutions;
- and contact and communication with client.

Alternative treatment options are usually available. Frequently, the best choices are those that work in concert with natural processes or are the least intrusive. Let's be mindful, however, that the capacity to choose from among alternatives is highly dependent upon accurate information.

By using this analogy, the public can come to understand the principles of PHC which are fairly simple in themselves, but complex in their application and implementation. In this context, the public can better accept the thoroughly integrated approach of PHC to plant care. PHC considers multiple tactics and relies primarily on environmental management measures — those that encourage plant reactions to change and maintain healthy, balanced growth, rather than emphasizing treatments for pests. Chemical applications in PHC, like drugs in human health care, are not "bad." They are, however, recognized as just one of the many tools utilized to promote plant health. In specific cases, they are required when other stress management tools have failed to meet client expectations. And now, as in human health care, we are more aware of the importance of minimal application rates, and the dangers of reliance on single chemical systems. The public can understand chemical dependencies in human health care, which now makes it easier to understand why overuse of chemicals in the landscape can be non-sustainable and potentially dangerous (due to pest resistance, buildup of toxic residues, or non-target effects such as preditors and ecological addiction).

This analogy is not only accurate, but represents an easy way for the PHC practitioner to translate the concept to the consumer in a familiar context. Arborists may encounter some of the same resistances that people have in terms of human health care. Some people will view chemical applications (like drugs) in any concentration to be potentially hazardous and unacceptable. In most instances, however, the parallel between human and plant health maintenance can be used to establish the diversity of tactics used in a logical perspective and understandable human terms.

Before moving on, let's return briefly to one's expectations of an HMO: ". . .a person can expect *personalized attention from a caring, responsive, and professional staff. . .*" In PHC absolutely nothing less will do. As will be discov-

Contact and communication are among the key elements of a successful PHC program.

PLANT HEALTH CARE (PHC): AN OVERVIEW / 3

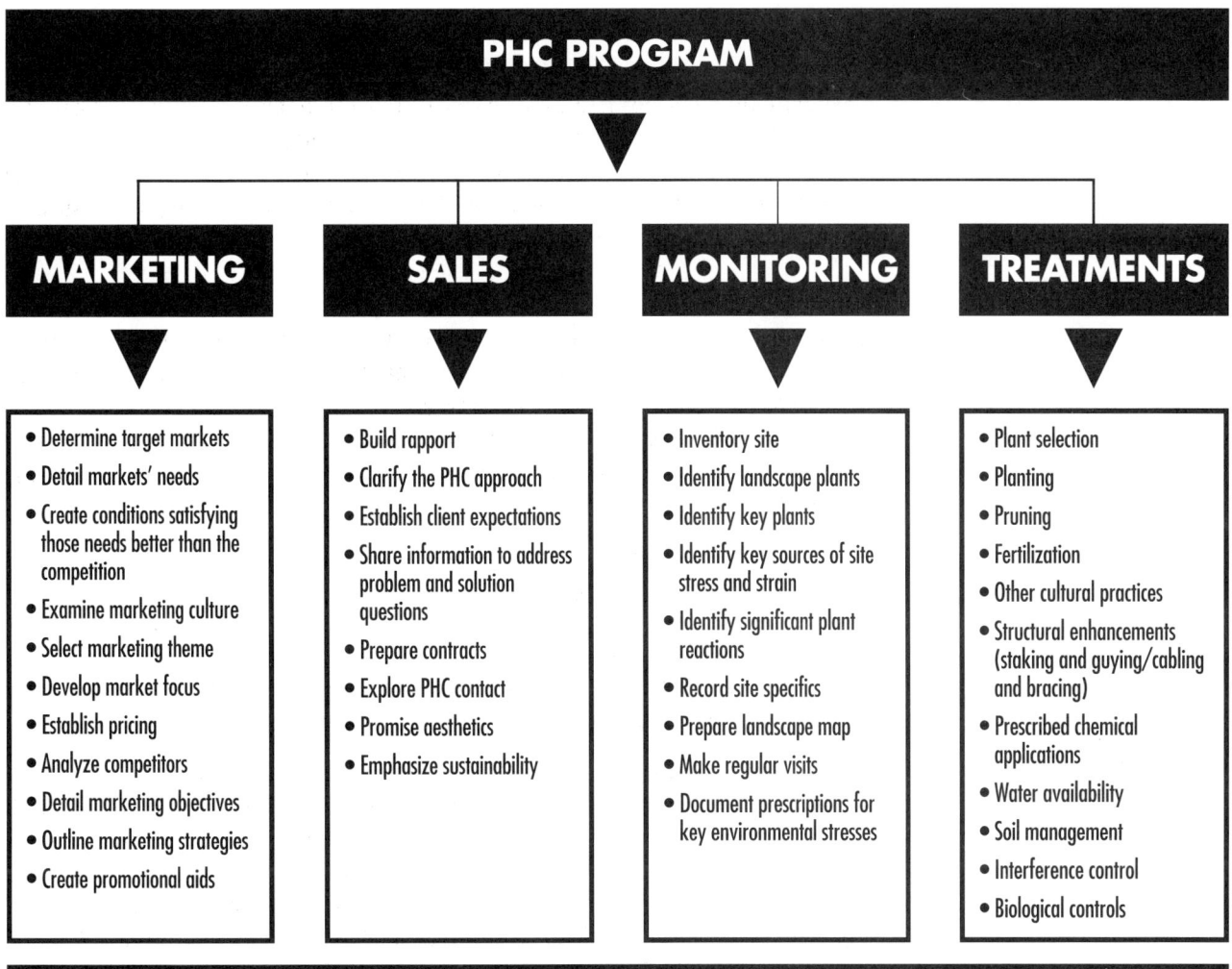

Figure 1 - 1. Key components, functions and activities of a PHC Program. Individual PHC practitioners will structure the program in a way that best fits their company and their market.

ered in Chapter 2, PHC consumers expect, in fact, demand, the same level of service as that of an HMO. Contact and communication are among the key elements of a successful PHC program.

PHC IS A CONTRACTUAL SERVICE

As with the HMO, PHC is a service in which people perceive value, have distinct expectations and provides contractual services. PHC is seen as a means to minimize many problems in the client's landscape by invigorating plants to strengthen their natural reactions to a changing growth environment. Clients appreciate the practitioner's ability to anticipate likely problems as well as discover and solve problems early by selecting from a broad spectrum of treatment options. Clients appreciate a professional's personal attention to client needs and desires as well as the plants. They appreciate receiving authoritative information, timely and credible action, and peace of mind regarding their landscapes.

Plant Health Care practitioners are *authoritative professionals* and must see themselves as such. When seeking services for human health, we search for authoritative professionals and are willing to *contract* for their services to help us maintain our health. There is little difference between human health and plant health in this matter.

Arboriculture has been touted as a *profession* for many years. We in the industry must increasingly see ourselves as authoritative professionals, act the part, and not be shy about contracts.

PHC: A NATURAL INTEGRATION

PHC should be an integral part of commercial plant care because it works and because it is profitable. It provides proactive plant care solutions which are long-term, environmentally-sensitive, and cost-effective.

PHC has the flexibility to rapidly evolve in response to previous treatments, climatic conditions, local regulations, and the knowledge level of the client. The specific blend of services and treatments offered by a PHC program will also evolve in response to client input and company resources and goals. Maximum benefits and profits over the long term can be produced if all PHC principles are applied. While the principles of PHC are uniform, individual programs will undoubtedly vary widely in appearance between companies. This variance may be due to local market conditions, financial resources, personnel resources, etc. Be that as it may, it bears repeating: *Maximum benefits and profits over the long term can be produced only when all PHC principles are consistently and diligently applied.*

REGULAR ON-SITE VISITS — A PHC IMPERATIVE

Informed decision-making requires monitoring. Monitoring provides opportunities for face-to-face dialogue with the client, which is essential for developing and maintaining strong client trust. Through periodic on-site customer service and monitoring visits, PHC:

Monitoring provides opportunities for face-to-face dialogue with the client. . .

- focuses on working simultaneously with the client and the plant.
- harmonizes with the level of client interest in plants and provides technical information in a context of client service.
- communicates to the client that problems are being anticipated and monitored.
- finds appropriate solutions to any problems identified using broad treatment options.
- prevents or minimizes many problems from getting started by invigorating the plant to strengthen its reactions to environmental changes.
- generates client confidence and keeps small problems from becoming client and/or plant crises.

Additionally, PHC can generate increased profits through regular on-site visits. Earned trust will reduce the cost of generating future sales, and may place the practitioner in a position of non-competitive pricing on future treatments. Regular monitoring and client dialogue can also lead to an increase in sales of add-on cultural treatments. These add-ons may include pruning, root crown inspections, mulching, fertilization, soil aeration, lawn care, irrigation system design and installation, and landscape design and renovation. Monitoring and informed decision making can also increase profits by reducing pesticide use and costs.

THE EVOLUTION OF PHC

Plant Health Care was derived from Integrated Pest Management (IPM). The emphasis in each system is different. PHC provides a focus on the individual plant and the management of the growing environment surrounding the plant. IPM provides prevention as an aspect of the entire management system, but does not focus on that aspect. IPM was originally designed for monoculture farming systems that had little plant diversity and a cropping-based guild of pests. The focus is not on keeping individual plants healthy, but on reducing pesticide use and maintaining a profitable yield on an area basis through diversification of management strategies.

Although the management strategies and theory behind IPM are applicable to agriculture, the focus on area management and profitable yield do not lend themselves well to landscape situations. Rather than refine IPM to fit the green industry and add confusion to the public's perception of IPM, the Plant Health Care Management System was created. PHC is, in part, an enhancement of IPM for landscape professionals. The IPM focus on management of pests and profitable yields has been enriched to a PHC focus on the individual plant, environmental management, and the client. Plant Health Care is the proactive approach to mantaining tree health through holistic cultural management. The goal of PHC is to maintain tree health by providing the proper growing environment for the plant.

Plant Health Care is the proactive approach to maintaining tree health through holistic cultural management.

Since PHC evolved from IPM, basic principles are shared. These principles include monitoring, developing thresholds, identifying key stress(es), cultural manipulation and plant resistance, and using multiple management options when necessary. These principles have been adapted in PHC to deal with the diversity of plants associated with the urban forest. Several other principles were added to PHC that are unique to urban and community forestry and associated plant care. These principles include: customer service as the driving force; the concept of key plants; and aesthetic, psychological, and environmental thresholds. All of these principles are necessary to deal with the diverse species of perennial plants in the landscape which have economic, aesthetic, emotional, and environmental functions and values.

Plant care is primarily a service business. It is the client who pays the bill for plant care treatments. PHC recognizes the importance of an informed client and balances customer service with the promotion of plant health. Practical benefits include improved communication between client and arborist, development of a high level of client confidence in the arborist, and reliance by the client on the professional expertise and integrity of the PHC practitioner.

A central principle of PHC is that multiple treatment options can be used to obtain positive results. PHC recognizes that a potential for an unhealthy plant exists and the professional may implement prescribed treatments to prevent a problem from getting started. If a problem does get started, but is identified early, low impact treatments can be used to solve a small problem at a low cost. However, if a problem becomes major, complementary treatments can be combined for increased effectiveness. Treatments may be passive, intended to (1) postpone action, gather more information, and re-evaluate the situation later or, (2) delay action until environmental conditions improve and can take care of the problem. Alternatively, treatments may be active, through improving environmental conditions or application of supplemental chemicals. Treatments may be used alone or in combination. Most effective results are obtained when treatments are organized into an integrated system. The best treatments can then be chosen for each specific situation.

KEY PLANT CONCEPT

The **key plant concept** prepares a list of plant species that are commonly affected by anticipated environmental stresses. Inspections and potential treatments should focus on those species clearly identified by client objectives or known to be biologically susceptable, as most likely having significant impact. Practical benefits of key plant status include increased selectivity of treatment, increased savings in time and money, and further enhancement of environmental quality.

Plants in the landscape have values that affect the amount of attention and treatment each will receive. Depending upon a plant's location in the landscape, its value can be higher than for other plants of the same species, size, and condition. If the client associates some special event with the plant, the subjective value of the plant may be much higher than the objective landscape value would indicate. PHC assesses the subjective and objective value of a plant and schedules preferential treatment for the higher value key plants. One practical benefit of the concept of key plants is allowance for optimum distribution of limited resources to those plants that are most valuable to the customer. In addition, it creates an opportunity for the PHC practitioner to reinforce key plant and key stress concepts as a means of changing the client's plant valuation process or increasing the amount of resources the client is willing to invest in plant care.

> *Plants in the landscape have values that affect the amount of attention and treatment each will receive.*

KEY STRESS CONCEPT

Another central principle of PHC is the **key stress concept**. Plants are influenced by many internal and external causes of stress and strain. Causes of stress can be classified as predominately physical, mechanical, biological, chemical, genetic, or ecological. All plants are in some way constrained by stress from reaching full expression of their genetic potential. Plant reactions to most stress components have been well-integrated into growth and development processes. Other stress components initiate plant reactions that can be seen as distinct symptoms. The results of all the many genetic and environmental interactions produce the plant that we see.

Knowledge of the key plant and key stress concepts provides an extremely powerful plant care management tool that dramatically improves efficiency. Advance knowledge of predicted stress levels for each species creates two benefits. First, it allows for advance planning and organization of treatments. Second, it improves timing of treatments and result evaluation. Advance planning may eliminate the need for supplemental treatments by selecting and planting species of plants that can tolerate stresses specific to a given environment. Advance planning also increases the time available to discuss appropriate alternative treatments with the client. As a result, plants are more likely to be kept healthy and attractive at less cost and with less environmental impact.

The diagnostic foundation of PHC is provided by the environmental sensing and reaction system of the plant. Plant reactions are genetically controlled and provide different responses from species to species. Failures of plant systems to properly respond and limit stress effects are the exceptions. In most instances, plant systems effectively react to environmental changes and the plant survives. Effectiveness of plant systems to react to environmental changes can be altered by changes in the growing conditions. In general, plants react more effectively and efficiently when growing conditions are optimal and the plants are healthy.

> *Knowledge of the key plant and key stress concepts provides an extremely powerful plant care management tool that dramatically improves efficiency.*

PLANT HEALTH CARE (PHC): AN OVERVIEW / 7

The key stress concept has tremendous practical impact. Existing problems can often be solved by improving growing conditions. This cultural manipulation may negate the need for supplemental chemical treatments which, in turn, enhances environmental quality, reduces costs and promotes long-term results.

Monitoring and manipulating a plant's reaction to environmental changes can effectively limit stress effects to small portions of the plant, or allow systemic stress to be managable. Plant reactions can compensate for stress to restore and maintain effective function. As a result of understanding and anticipating plant reactions, treatment may be postponed when stress is not deemed significant. By developing monitoring thresholds, we can determine when management action is necessary to prevent significant damage. A *threshold* is the intensity or extent of a tree's reaction to stress where additional treatments should be activated.

The establishment of threshold levels requires foreknowledge of plant reactions, growing conditions, and associated key stresses.

The establishment of threshold levels requires foreknowledge of plant reactions, growing conditions and associated key stresses. Threshold establishment also requires an assessment of the amount of stress symptom expression acceptable to the client. Thresholds are dynamic and vary with plant age and health, effectiveness of plant reactions against a specific pest, growing conditions, client expectations and history of previous treatments. Thresholds also vary with the amount of confidence the client places in the PHC practitioner and the key plant status. Within the context of the urban forest, threshold categories are economic, aesthetic, ecological, biological and psychological. PHC invigorates the plant, strengthens plant reactions, and raises the knowledge level of the client. As a result, many supplemental chemical treatments can be postponed or eliminated.

Determining if a threshold level has been reached requires the gathering of information through regular monitoring of plant vitality and appearance, growing conditions, stress levels, and customer perceptions. Based upon the information gathered and accumulated over time, supplemental treatments can be evaluated and selected. Monitoring continues after initial treatments to determine the effectiveness of treatments and the need for modified treatments or additional manipulations of the plant and environment.

Use of more invasive, non-targeted, or artificial treatments are reserved as a last resort. These treatments are utilized only when plant reactions are not effective, and monitoring has shown that the stress symptom expression levels have reached a management threshold. A major criterion in selecting a potential supplemental treatment is the degree of environmental impact it carries. PHC always emphasizes management that produces the least environmental disruption to meet client objectives.

CHAPTER SUMMARY

- PHC is a people and plant concept. PHC provides an effective and profitable approach that balances the needs of people and the needs of plants within an environmental context.
- Supplemental chemical treatments are reduced by manipulating growing conditions to enhance plant health and stimulate effective and efficient reactions by the plant to environmental conditions.
- Specific principles include customer service as a driving force; monitoring; developing economic, aesthetic, psychological, biological, and ecological thresholds; identifying key stresses, key plants; preventing problems through

The challenge of PHC is great, but the benefit of healthy landscape plants and an improved environment, at less cost, is even greater.

cultural manipulation and plant resistance; and using multiple management options if necessary.
- PHC matches the strength of the treatment to the severity of the problem within an environmental context. Practical benefits of this principle of alternative treatments include reduction in cost of treatment, enhancement of environmental quality, and flexibility in selecting options.
- While PHC principles are simple, applications may be made complex due to the wide variety of plant requirements, client inputs, societal needs, and company goals.
- PHC practitioners must learn what constitutes ideal and acceptable conditions for thousands of species, communicate the need for actions effectively to the client, and then generate and maintain plant health given the management constraints present.
- The challenge of PHC is great, but the benefit of healthy landscape plants and an improved environment, at less cost, is even greater.

CHAPTER

2

PHC Marketing: The Consumers

INTRODUCTION

The Plant Health Care Management System (PHC) was created as a concept that would help plant care professionals balance the needs of plants with the needs of people. On the one hand PHC is holistic, professionally-responsible, technically-advanced, preventive maintenance plant care which can be used on one plant or a whole landscape. But at the same time PHC also creates a sophisticated method to respond to the needs of the clients who will contract for plant care services. The basic steps of a PHC program orchestrate the development and maintenance of an on-going relationship between the plant care professional and client.

This chapter will thoroughly acquaint professionals with the consumers of plant care services. To know and understand the consumer is the first step to persuade the consumer to contract for PHC. That understanding provides businesses with solid information on which to build successful marketing strategies. Chapter 3 offers general company-specific business considerations and Chapter 4 is devoted to actually crafting an individualized PHC marketing plan.

WHO ARE TREE CARE CONSUMERS?

Tree care consumers are quite distinct from those in the public mainstream.

In recent years, a series of national and regional studies have been conducted examining the beliefs and perceptions of landscape and tree care consumers. Rather than report the findings of each study in turn, what follows is a combination of the results in a single summary of reliable conclusions. We can begin this summary by first challenging the belief, held by many professionals, that the consumer market is best reflected by the general public. Our data suggest that this is far from the truth. On almost every critical dimension, current and prospective tree care consumers are quite distinct from those in the public mainstream. Figure 2-1 illustrates just how distinct this consumer group is.

Tree care consumers tend to be older, more highly educated, more likely to own a home, more likely to live longer in that home, and likely to have a larger number of mature trees on their property than do other citizens. Most impressive, tree care consumers are affluent, even when compared to other

10 / THE PLANT HEALTH CARE MANAGEMENT SYSTEM

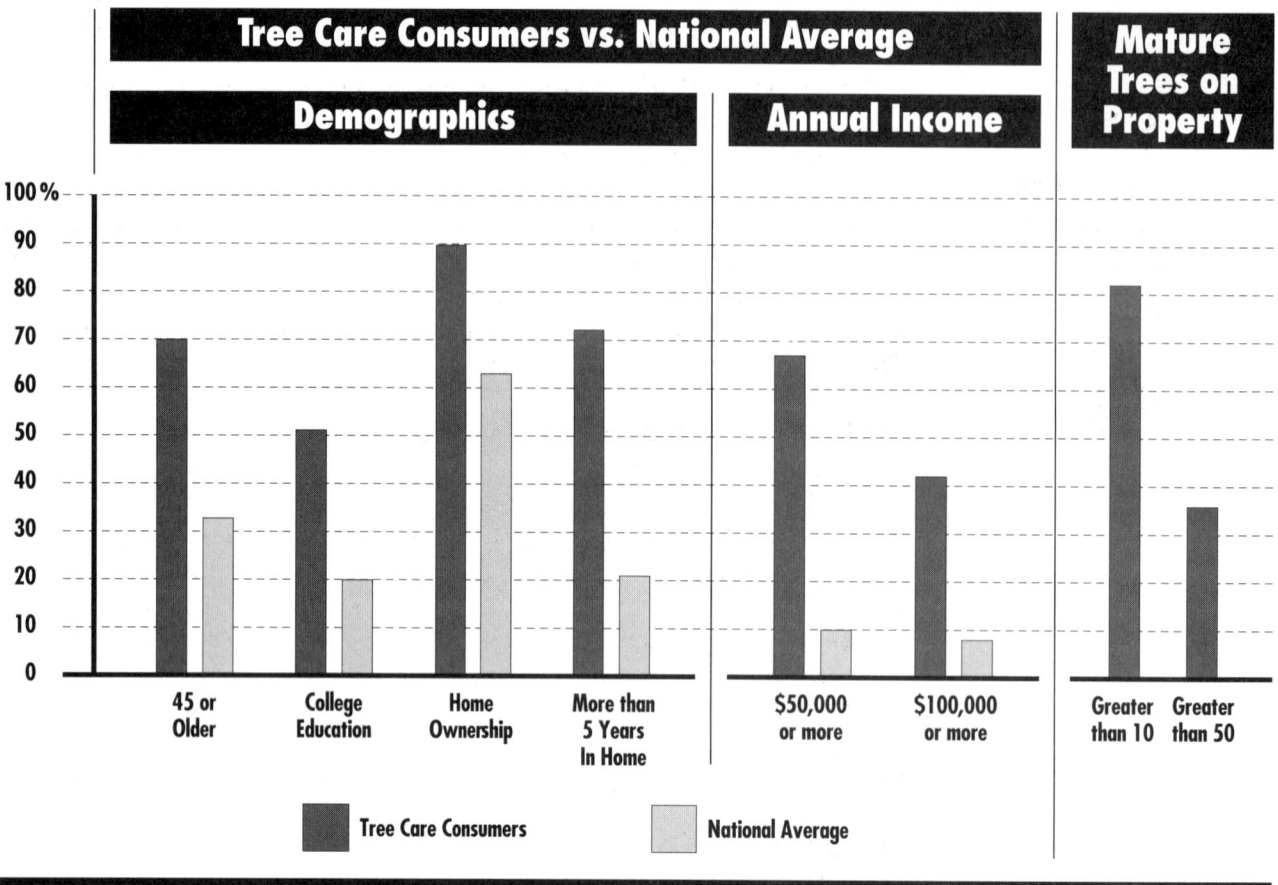

Figure 2-1. Characteristics of tree care consumers. (1992 Statistics)

well-to-do consumers. As one might expect, such a unique segment of the population also holds beliefs and expectations about tree and landscape professionals that differ from other consumers.

TREE CARE CONSUMERS ARE NOT ENVIRONMENTALISTS

If one reads recent national polls by the Gallup or Roper organizations, the conclusion that the public is environmentally-conscious is hard to deny. In fact, in one study by Gallup, more than 75 percent of Americans polled reported that they considered themselves "environmentalists." Surprisingly, on the whole, tree care consumers are neither average nor environmentally-concerned. Consumers of landscape services desire the best looking property possible for the money they are willing to spend. Environmental concern is left to the arborist.

Consistent with this attitude, when asked to rate their opinion about the use of chemicals in blanket sprayings to control pests, consumers reported only a slight disfavor with this approach. The average score along a 1 to 7 continuum, where 1 reflects disfavor and 7 reflects favor, was 3.8 (Fig. 2-2). In other words, contrary to popular belief, targeted tree care customers do not strongly oppose the use of chemical pesticides in cover sprays.

When consumers are told about more environmentally-sensitive methods of stress management and that these methods are sometimes more expensive than traditional techniques, (this cost factor is not specified), they generally resist such methods. When asked specifically if alternative methods were worth any additional costs, the average response of 4.3 was only slightly above the neutral mark [4.0 is neutral, 1 represents "not worth additional costs" and 7

Tree care consumers are neither average nor environmentally-concerned.

There appears to be a strong bias for fast-acting methods of plant care.

represents "worth the additional costs"] (Fig. 2-2). Although property managers and residential customers are not environmentally-conscious, they do perceive strong social responsibilities. In other words, they care what others think, especially neighbors. Property managers and homeowners who see themselves under scrutiny from neighbors, or the public, are much more likely to hold unfavorable attitudes toward pesticide usage.

Only two other stable beliefs surfaced regarding customer perceptions of alternative methods of pest control. On the positive side, respondents believe that alternative methods are less toxic and therefore less harmful to the environment and to humans. Negatively, property owners and managers viewed the effects of alternative methods as taking far longer than traditional methods. There appears to be a strong bias for fast-acting methods.

TREE CARE CONSUMERS DESIRE INFORMATION

Because PHC involves a range of treatment methods, we asked respondents to rate their interest in information related to the trees on their property. Figure 2-3 summarizes the average ratings for six topics along a continuum ranging from 1 to 10, where 10 represents a great desire to know: (1) species identification, (2) maintenance requirements for individual trees and shrubs, (3) pest problems associated with trees, (4) health of individual trees and shrubs, (5) suggestions for tree plantings, and (6) monetary or replacement value of trees. The high marks in the categories of pest problems (7.8), health of individual trees (7.4), and maintenance requirements for individual trees (7.0) bodes well for PHC. Customers clearly desire information consistent with a PHC approach.

CONSUMERS HAVE LOW EXPECTATIONS REGARDING TREE CARE SERVICES

When asked to think of tree care companies, consumers conjured three primary images. First, they identify tree care and other landscape professionals with the construction industry. Tree care professionals are generally thought to be blue-collar workers with limited expertise. Consistent with this image, consumers associate tree care professionals with large trucks and equipment. Sec-

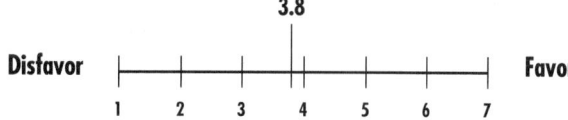

Figure 2 - 2. Reflections of environmental attitudes of tree care consumers with regard to usage of chemicals.

12 / THE PLANT HEALTH CARE MANAGEMENT SYSTEM

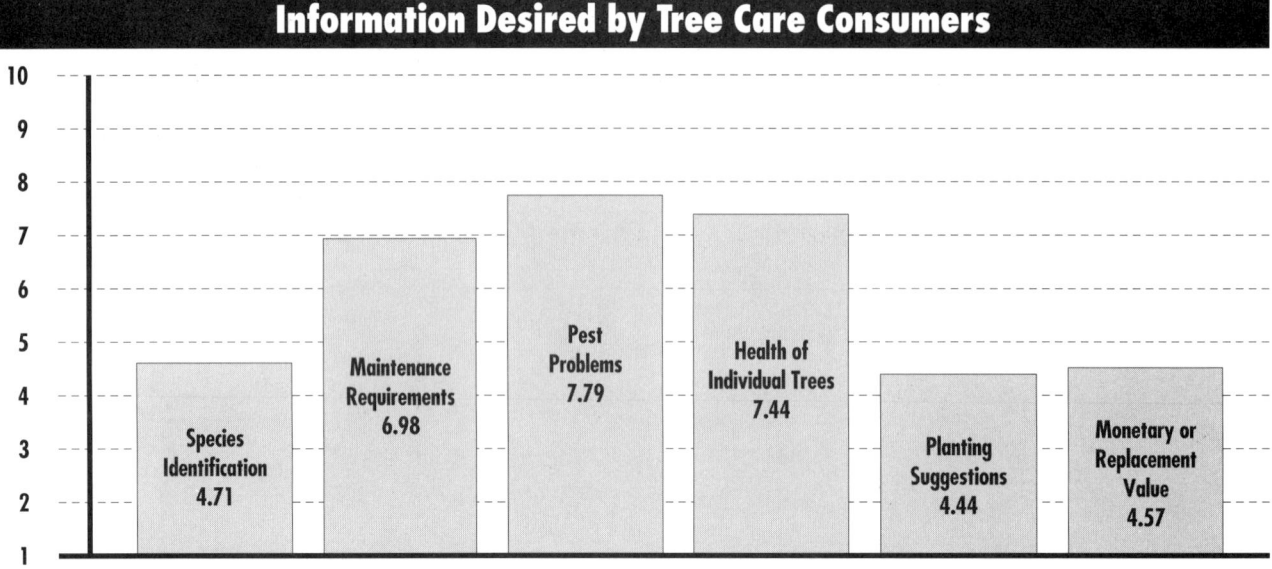

Figure 2 - 3. Average scores across sample from survey of six topics of interest of tree care consumers.

ond, although they cannot classify this equipment (a bucket truck means no more or less than a large chipper), consumers presume that tree care professionals are expert at operating this heavy machinery. Interestingly, industry professionals are not seen as possessing the same level of expertise with trees. Third, consumers expect inexperienced, impersonal and inconsistent service from tree care companies. Although they hold positive perceptions about tree care services, these perceptions tend to be global or general in nature. Negative perceptions held by consumers, on the other hand, appear to be specific and stable.

These images and patterns exist for consumers who value and consumers who do not value tree care services. For example, in several studies we asked consumers to rate the importance of tree care maintenance to ensure tree health. The average response score along a continuum ranging from 1 to 7, where 1 reflects little importance and 7 high importance, was 4.5 with a great deal of variation. In other words, this average is not very meaningful. Generally, respondents either believed that tree care maintenance is essential or that it is of minimal importance. The key point, however, is that both groups held low expectations about tree care services.

We can provide a more detailed picture of the beliefs toward tree care services (Fig. 2-4). Respondents across the studies reported five primary beliefs or reasons for contracting with a tree care service. First, a tree care service is best prepared to deal with large tree pruning and tree removal. Second, tree care services are superior for enhancing the physical appearance of a property. Third, ridding trees of pests is best handled by a service. Fourth, a tree care service saves time for the property owner or manager. Fifth, the knowledge possessed by tree care experts enables them to solve difficult problems and to prevent future tree damage.

On the negative side, customers see four primary drawbacks to contracting with a tree care service. First, consumers believe that services are costly. Second, a stable belief exists that tree companies provide poor and/or inconsistent service. Property owners and managers who hold this belief are also likely to believe that the seasonal help utilized by tree service companies are inexperienced and unknowledgeable. Third, customers view the lack of a guarantee

Consumer Perceptions of Tree Care Providers

Positive	Negative
• Arborists are best prepared to deal with large trees (pruning and removal)	• Tree care service is too expensive
• Arborists enhance the physical appearance of a property	• Companies provide poor and/or inconsistent service
• Tree experts are best at handling pest problems	• Employees are inexperienced and unknowledgeable
• Tree services save time	• No guarantee system for planting or treatment
• Arborists can prevent future damage to my trees	• I cannot judge the service quality I receive
	• I cannot differentiate between companies

Figure 2 - 4. Common perceptions of tree care providers held by consumers.

system (planting and treatment) to diminish the value of the service. Fourth, customers do not know how to choose a service. Even property managers reported that they had no way to judge the merits of one service over another.

MYSTERY OF CONSUMER DESIRES

Despite the clarity afforded by earlier research findings, consumers of plant care services frequently seem mysterious and idiosyncratic. One customer wants the latest high-tech treatment strategy, while another longs for blanket sprays. One customer desires a pest-free landscape, while the next door neighbor wants to avoid the drift. While research displays a wide variety of consumer concerns and requirements relative to plant care services, it also shows consumers to be remarkably consistent in their desire for three things: contact, information, and aesthetics.

These are three basic features that every arborist must offer a plant care client. But before reading about those three features, let's look at three examples from the trail of research that led up to this understanding.

MYSTERY STUDY # 1: DEBORAH AND SAM

Deborah is a research chemist and Sam is in real estate sales. Combined income: $110,000. Home: 30-year-old colonial. Plantings range from five to thirty years old. Total investment in house and grounds: $250,000.

Views on Plant Care: Both believe that plants require care, but each differs in expectations on what such a service should provide. Sam wants his driveway lined with beautiful plants. He wants to pay his money and purchase the assurance that things will be taken care of. He wants peace of mind and an aesthetically pleasing property. Period. Deborah, on the other hand, wants to know more about what she is paying for. She enjoys learning about plants. When she finds an arborist who will provide her with information that demystifies the process of plant care, she will consider signing up for service.

So far no arborist has been satisfactory to both of them. Deborah and

Sam are plant care consumers. Yet neither one has factored holistic or non-holistic plant care into the discussions on the selection of an arborist. They remain to be educated on that point. For the moment Sam only knows that he wants beauty and the peace of mind that accompanies beauty. Deborah knows that she wants personal contact and information. Beauty is a given. Yet Sam and Deborah, beneath the surface of their differences, are both in the market for the same thing. That is the mystery.

But what about Susan? An average, single working woman. What could be mysterious about her?

MYSTERY STUDY # 2: SUSAN

Susan earns $40,000 a year and lives alone. The one huge old beech tree which shades her entire house showed alarming signs of decline last summer.

Views on Plant Care: Uneasy thoughts of chemical sprays came to mind when Susan thought of arbor care. Yet she fully expected that those chemicals would save her beech tree. Her confidence was so great that, while the potential costs concerned her, she had already decided that—with the "right" arborist, she would have her sickly foundation plantings treated as well.

She cared for the beech tree. And the tree seemed to respond. But her arborist never got wind of the extra work. That particular arborist treated her as though she really didn't understand. The arborist just wasn't the right one. That is the mystery of Susan.

Is the common thread that binds these consumers visible yet? Consider. Susan does not earn the money that Deborah and Sam do. She is not in the market for an arborist to treat her entire landscape on an on-going basis. But her basic requirements are nearly identical to Deborah's and Sam's. The mystery is really not a mystery at all. In reality, the consumers are practically shouting the answer. There are three things that consumers require of their arborist. Three things, which join in combination to create one very important item. One more case study should make the point clear.

MYSTERY STUDY #3: DIANE AND BILL

Diane and Bill inherited money, ten acres and a large Victorian home.

Views on Plant Care: Diane doesn't want excuses, she wants results. Imperfection disturbs her. She appreciates that her arborist routinely consults her on her opinions and consequently maintains their property to perfection. Bill, however, used to regard plant care as almost superfluous before he became interested in the old oak tree at the corner of the property. When he was still living, his father would sit under the tree and talk about old times.

In one of the frequent conversations with Bill and Diane, their arborist learned of Bill's passion for the oak tree and now, when sending treatment summaries that follow each visit, the arborist makes it a point to include information on the culture and folklore of oaks — much to Bill's delight. Providing useful and interesting information to Bill and Diane has been a long-standing habit. But until this point, only Diane had commented on the material. With the discovery of Bill's passion for the oak tree, their arborist has struck a chord with Bill as well.

Bill and Diane's arborist has cracked the code, learning on the job what the research has proved empirically. The three features that consumers especially value from their arborist are contact, information and aesthetics.

Contact. The desire to converse with the person in whose hands one entrusts the care of some extremely valuable assets. The quite

Consumers desire Contact, Information, and Aesthetics

Beautiful plants might mean wealth, achievement, heritage or social standing to a consumer, — or perhaps just pure pleasure.

natural desire to form and develop bonds of empathy, trust, and understanding.

Information. It could be simple curiosity. It could be that consumers appreciate an arborist who takes the time to stop and consider their special needs, an arborist who provides them with the kind of information that keeps them abreast of developments in their landscape. The fact remains that tree care consumers have a strong appetite for information.

Aesthetics. Beautiful plants might mean wealth, achievement, heritage or social standing to the consumer, — or perhaps just pure pleasure.

Add these things together and find that the sum total of these three features is the quality that consumers want most from their arborist. They desire a meaningful, long term relationship. What the research clearly shows is that consumers most value a long term relationship with an arborist who displays a commitment to people as well as to the plants on the property.

By establishing contact in an atmosphere of openness, by initiating and maintaining an on-going dialogue that is supported by the flow of useful information and a willingness to listen, by delivering on the promise of healthy and beautiful plants, the arborist can sow the seeds of trust with the client that will grow into a working relationship which will bear fruit for many years to come.

CONSUMER PROFILES

Tree care consumers can be divided into three types or profiles: Contact-driven, Information-driven, and Aesthetically-driven.

Contact, information and the continued health and beauty of plants are the essential elements that form the backbone of the special kind of relationships nurtured by Plant Health Care. An understanding and a sensitivity to the issues that are most important to the consumer is a critical part of opening, and then developing the dialogue that will continue across the years. Research suggests that tree care consumers can be divided into three types or profiles similar to the dimensions presented above and illustrated in Figure 2-5. These profiles highlight the unique qualities and beliefs of consumers. Read the profiles below with an eye toward the kinds of beliefs that motivate the consumers in your business. Recognize the fact that these profiles are ideal-types. No one person will likely embody any given profile. Rather, consumers will often have a combination of beliefs that defies typecasting. The point is to become aware that the beliefs exist within clients and to develop strategies that exploit their presence.

The **Contact-driven Consumer** is a non-environmentally-minded individual who views trees as a resource, a commodity, things to be maintained. Consistent with this view, the Contact-driven consumer believes that trees will sustain themselves if they are treated properly. As a caretaker, this person will have an interest in finding a competent professional to relieve the burden of this care. This individual highly values service, and in order to please such a client, the arborist must stand behind the service provided, squarely addressing any problem arising. Pest problems are the arborist's concern. By contracting for service, this individual feels that he or she has fulfilled his or her obligation to the landscape.

The **Information-driven Consumer** is more environmentally concerned than his/her counterparts. Trees are symbolic of social values; they represent a concern for the future and a caring for the planet. These consumers view the landscape as a complex living system where they are stewards tending to the needs of the land. Consistent with this view, they would prefer not to disturb the natural processes, preferring not to harm anything, including pests, unless it was absolutely necessary. Of the three profiles, the Information-driven Consumer is the most price conscious. Demanding value for their money, the guarantee of work to be done is essential for this group. Economy along with a credibility based upon information, as well as the presence of guarantees, will prove the major selling points for these consumers.

The **Aesthetically-driven Consumer** considers property to be an investment and views the landscape as an asset or a liability. Consequently, trees represent wealth to this person, but they also tie into a desired sense of history and permanence. This client is frequently status conscious, especially when established in a recently purchased home. He/she will care what neighbors think and this may possibly translate into an attitude of social responsibility. On the other hand, this person possesses a clear idea of how things should be and has little patience for service and treatment that does not produce immediate results. Pests, all pests, must be eradicated to satisfy this need for perfection. While promises of effects will help sell this person, proven results will succeed in modifying expectations and full acceptance of the ideas of a Plant Health Care program.

MOVING FORWARD

While Plant Health Care offers responsible tree care emphasizing a reduction in the usage of pesticides, the fact of the matter is that most consumers will not respond to a marketing campaign that emphasizes this environmental ethic as

Consumer Profiles

CONTACT-DRIVEN	INFORMATION-DRIVEN	AESTHETICALLY-DRIVEN
• Status conscious (often new homeowners) • Trees represent history, longevity, wealth • Property is an investment • Service and treatment must have immediate effects • Pests must be eradicated (all pests) **SELLING POINTS:** • *Promises of Effects* • *Proven Results*	Environmentally concerned • Price-conscious • Trees are symbolic of social values • Landscape is a complex, living system • Guarantee of work is essential • Don't harm anything unless it is necessary (including pests) **SELLING POINTS:** • *Credibility* • *Price*	• Environmentally indifferent • Service-conscious • Trees are a resource, a commodity • Trees will sustain themselves if treated properly • Caretaker view of landscape • Arborist must stand behind service—address problems • Pest problems are arborists' concern **SELLING POINTS:** • *Professionalism* • *Service Package*

Figure 2 - 5. **There are three generalized types or profiles of plant health care consumers.**

well as they might respond to one that offers the promise of contact, information and aesthetics. Research clearly shows that the typical plant care client has no strong bias against the use of chemicals on his or her property. The findings further show that clients are far less likely to be motivated by environmental sensitivity than they are by their interest in beautiful plants.

Plant Health Care is tailored to meet the needs of the consumer and can become a powerful tool for generating new sales within an existing client base. At the same time, it can reach out to previously untapped markets. Facets of PHC must be presented in such a way as to create certain perceptions in the mind of the targeted audience. As these perceptions build, one upon another, they become a part of an argument or a persuasion. Properly constructed and tailored to fit the requirements of potential clients, they plant the seeds of need and desire. These seeds ultimately lead to sales.

Without question, consumers strongly desire what Plant Health Care has to offer. Understanding how a long-term relationship can profit all parties is but the first step toward creating or expanding a Plant Health Care program. Study and practice will bring immediate benefits but more critical still, for the overall development of a business, is the creation of a Marketing Plan that will effectively translate these understandings to your business. Mapping out goals, developing strategies and creating client expectations to live up to will help to create the kind of stability in your company that will attract clients whose interests lie in a long-term relationship. The time you spend developing your relationship with your *own* company will repay itself many times over.

Without question, consumers strongly desire what Plant Health Care has to offer.

CHAPTER SUMMARY

- Understanding the consumer is essential for persuading them to contract for Plant Health Care.
- Typical tree care consumers are older, better educated, and more financially secure than the general public. They are more likely to own their own homes, live in them longer, and have large numbers of mature trees on their property.
- Although consumers have positive general perceptions about tree care services, they expect inexperienced, impersonal, and inconsistent service from tree care companies. Violate these expectations in positive ways.
- Consumers of plant care services consistently desire contact, information, and aesthetics. These are the backbone of the ongoing relationship between PHC professionals and customers.
- Consumers typically fit one of three profiles: Contact-driven, Information-driven, or Aesthetically-driven. Become aware of consumer beliefs, understand them, and develop strategies that exploit their presence. There are specific selling points for each consumer profile.

CHAPTER

3

PHC Marketing: Strategies and Planning

INTRODUCTION

Implementation of the Plant Health Care Management System is a complex undertaking. Selling, monitoring, diagnosing, staffing, record keeping, and information resourcing are all areas that will require significant attention when putting systems into place. Honing marketing skills and developing solid business plans and strategies, however, may be the most vital part of implementing a *successful* PHC program. Many managers will find that PHC requires, to a greater or lesser degree, a departure from the way they have traditionally done business. Additionally, changes and trends in the business environment of the green industry must be taken into account.

The goal of this chapter is to stimulate, not teach. It poses more questions than answers. It presents business and marketing considerations that relate to implementing the Plant Health Care Management System. Chapter 4 is designed to guide you in creating your own PHC marketing plan.

FROM THE PRESENT TO THE FUTURE

We cannot effectively plan for the future without examining the issues and trends facing us today.

The decision to implement a PHC service, or not, depends largely on the short- and long-term goals of your company. Since you are reading this book, we will assume that:

- you are already servicing landscape needs of one sort or another,
- you are familiar with other landscape care businesses in your locale which offer services similar to yours,
- you are aware of current (and the trend toward increasing) governmental regulations regarding pesticides.

We cannot effectively plan for the future without examining the issues and trends facing us today. The green industry, like many, is feeling the proverbial "winds of change." We can start the examination by asking: Who is going to be doing what and how in the future and what trends are we already seeing? We are seeing lawn care companies that have specialized in fertilizing and pest control now including tree care as a secondary service. We see commercial tree care companies branching into lawn care as a secondary service. We are seeing

19

expansion and diversification of services offered by all types of landscape businesses. There are no clear-cut deliniations of services offered within the various segments of the green industry. The care of trees, for example, is no longer the exclusive domain of commercial tree care companies, even though they still possess the most expertise and experience. Today they are joined by almost every other subset of the green industry, including garden centers, nurseries, landscape contractors, etc. Each of these groups is in a position to add services which they had previously not offered. Many businesses within these groups are concerning themselves with the plants that PHC is designed to care for. Most claim to be experts in plant care, and, indeed, many are. Some, unfortunately, are untrained and inexperienced but are doing it nonetheless.

Because of dilution of primary service markets, some experts feel that if companies don't expand, and diversify, they'll become dinosaurs over time. Take the timeless example from Theodore Levitt's "Marketing Myopia[1]." While expanding on the subject of management failure, Levitt noted that the demise of railroads in the U.S. was not caused because the need for passenger and freight transportation had declined. Actually, the need had grown enormously. It was not caused because the need was filled by cars, trucks, or airplanes. It was caused by the need *not* being filled by the railroads themselves. They thought they were in the *railroad* business, not the *transportation* business! It never occured to them to get into the trucking or airline business as a natural adjunct to the rail business. They were once *transportation* giants with tremendous resources. Railroad management lacked vision.

Historically, industries experience growth, maturity, and ultimate decline. Only consumer-oriented industries that continue to evolve to meet the needs of the marketplace stay alive. Today we're inclined to think "tree care industry" or "lawn care industry." Current trends could be indicating an imminent evolution into the "Landscape Services Industry" where individual companies will choose which services under this umbrella they wish to provide. Are the winners going to be the companies that have broadened their lines of services? Good question and here's some more. Does remaining *status quo* mean growth has stopped? When growth stops, are decline and ultimate demise inevitable? Are we myopic when it comes to increased governmental regulation of chemical use in the landscape? Should we be looking to see who's making inroads into our primary service areas — and how and why? Are there ways to embrace, rather than isolate, competition so as to foster cooperation between businesses within the industry?

In terms of business planning, it does not really matter where we are coming from or what we are doing today. It does not matter what "industry" we think we are in today. It is tomorrow that counts when devising a business plan and vision is the key. Certainly, the mix of services we can and should offer is something we should examine even if, in the end, we decide to change nothing. We will at the very least have a better understanding of where we are and a better idea of where we are going. What the "green industry" as a whole will look like in the future depends on the collective vision of each company's management team today.

A possible answer to one of the questions above is: Yes, many of us are myopic when it comes to increased governmental regulations regarding chemical use in the environment. The trend is apparent and perhaps no other single factor will have more influence on the way businesses [can and must] operate in the future.

Many observers firmly believe that the practice of holistic landscape care, such as Plant Health Care is an imperative for the progressive landscape care

What the green industry will look like in the future depends on the collective vision of each company's management team today.

[1]This article originally appeared in *The Harvard Business* Review in September-October, 1975.

PHC MARKETING: STRATEGIES AND PLANNING / 21

companies of the future. And why not? This book will demonstrate that PHC, when well-managed:
- accommodates increased customer service,
- incorporates a holistic approach to plant care,
- reduces reliance on pesticides,
- fosters healthy, beautiful landscapes, and
- provides an opportunity for substantial profits.

Considering these features of Plant Health Care and looking at all the alternative methods of doing business in an evolving industry and a changing world, one could make a strong argument for adoption of PHC.

Our goal has been to heighten awareness that industries are ever-changing — none that survive are static. Family-run full-service corner grocery stores have practically vanished. They were replaced by supermarkets which are now being replaced by super supermarkets while the convenience store has found its own market niche. The price of gasoline doubled overnight in the early seventies. Most cars suddenly got smaller, lighter, and travelled more miles to the gallon. Washable synthetic fabrics diminished the once-booming dry cleaning industry. VCRs have changed the movie theater industry. It seems that this list could go on forever.

The landscape industry is only beginning to evolve. What changes are in store? Time will tell, but major changes probably won't happen overnight. For example, it is likely that well-equipped, experienced commercial tree care companies will continue to dominate aerial pruning, cabling and bracing and removals of larger mature trees. Should a general landscape contractor, not currently handling these services but having an interest in trees, gear up to handle them? Could the fostering of cooperation among existing competitors be beneficial?

Bottom line: When developing current business and marketing plans, keep in mind that the mix of services provided by the various players in the landscape industry is changing. Establishing a PHC practice requires a marketing plan which must include a realistic view of all competition, present and future. Now let's move on to marketing.

> *...the mix of services provided by the various players in the landscape industry is changing.*

GENERAL MARKETING REVIEW

Marketing, in the simplist definition, is the exchange of value for value. In other words, two parties perceive each other to have something of value the other would like. Typically one party has services they are willing to exchange for money. The other party (with the means to pay) perceives the services to be of sufficient value that they will pay to receive them. Thus we have demand and subsequent exchange, or marketing. Let's clarify terminology before moving on:

Marketing focuses on the needs of the buyer, building awareness of needs, satisfying those needs through services, and the activities associated with creating and delivering those services.

Selling focuses on the needs of the seller to convert services into cash.

Demand for services is created by consumers having both the means and inclination to buy. Inclination to buy comes from perceived value. Perceived value comes in part from how well the benefits are sold and the confidence

> *Perceived value comes in part from how well the benefits are sold and the confidence that those benefits can be delivered.*

those benefits can be delivered. When we apply this to PHC, we're selling two things. Contracted plant health maintenance is a new concept to many prospective clients, so we must sell the benefits of its services as it applies to a specific property. We must then convince the consumer of our ability to deliver those benefits. Once sold and satisfactorily delivered during a season, PHC benefits become known-quantities and client satisfaction eases the burden of "reselling" in subsequent years.

The client must, in subtle ways, be reminded at every opportunity of the benefits of Plant Health Care. For example: "Its a good thing we caught this (problem) now before it got out of hand", or "We might be seeing a problem starting on (this or that) so we'll be keeping a close eye on it." Note that *subtle* is the key here. While all employees having contact with clients should be encouraged to talk up the benefits of PHC, caution should be taken against any statements that could be construed as arrogance.

Why such emphasis on constant selling? Since contracted care for woody plants is new to most clients, they need confirmation that PHC is serving them well. Moreover, it will take a while for most to see PHC as a beneficial necessity rather than a luxury. Should there be a period of inflation, or worse, a recession, pursestrings may be tightened. People tend to spend for necessities and cut back on luxuries during such periods. The more done to reinforce that significant assets are being protected, the more necessary that protection becomes. The best prospect for next year's contract is the client that *knows* he or she is being well-served today!

YOUR MARKETING MISSION

There seems to be an endless flow of self-help articles and books covering subjects of physical and emotional health, family matters, work practices, etc. Have you ever finished reading one of these treasures that someone took the time to organize and write for you, laid it down and said, "Gee, I knew that!?" It's quite common for us to think we're learning something new while reading, only to finish and realize that we actually already "knew" the material. It was the lack of organization in our minds that made it somewhat obscure.

Our mission must be reflected in all we say and do.

Believe it or not, our company's mission often falls prey to the same syndrome. We find ourselves in business for a variety of reasons, almost all of which are related to financial and psychological needs and desires within us. Therefore, our motives are usually self-serving and certainly financial gain takes a back seat to no other motive. Once a business has been established, however, the company must declare its mission. What is your company's mission? To make money? To take care of the employees and their families? No! These are by-products of a successful business. The mission of the service business must be the successful delivery of specific beneficial services to a specific market through a specific means. It is imperative that we establish a mission statement and not waver from its execution. It must be known to all, employees and clients alike. Our mission must be reflected in all we say and do.

Perhaps you've heard the story of Henry Ford's early mission statement. Bear in mind that this is the man credited with perfecting the assembly line as we know it today. The little known fact is that his marketing genius preceded his manufacturing genius. Henry took a look at the automobile industry, its products, and its markets. While he saw a tremendous potential market, the price of cars was such that the average person couldn't afford one. He then declared his intent to build and sell autos for five hundred dollars each, which was significantly lower than existing prices. His mission: to provide transportation to people of average means by offering a reliable automobile at a price they could afford. Henry Ford stated his mission and delivered on it. His mission was never to perfect the assembly line. It simply became the means which helped fulfill his mission. The assembly line, and his fame and fortune were by-products of a much larger vision.

The company's mission must be market-focused, well thought out and you must be able to declare it succinctly. You must know whom you are going to serve, how you are going to benefit them, and by what means you are going to make it happen. Sound planning requires a sound, well-focused mission.

AN OBJECTIVE LOOK AT SUBJECTIVE ISSUES

Let's take a look at one final matter before moving on to your marketing plan. Your Plant Health Care service will provide an opportunity to market a wide range of services packaged as one service. A well-implemented PHC program provides clients with the three things they value most:

- PHC provides *contact* — through regular property inspections, updates on changes, and landscape needs yet to be addressed.
- PHC provides the client with *information* — so they can be active participants in decision making regarding their landscape.
- PHC provides *aesthetics* — clients depend on your service to contribute to the beauty of their property by keeping their plants healthy.

This all sounds simple enough — Plant Health Care will meet the most important needs of your clients. In reality, however, each client is different from others to some degree. *Personnel factored into a marketing plan must be people-oriented and be able to read individual clients.*

- How much contact is enough without being too much?
- How much information will a client want? Will an individual want to know everything about a problem, just want to hear about solutions, or expect lessons in biology?
- What does aesthetics mean to a given client? How much beauty does the client expect? What will it cost your company to satisfy their expectations and is the client prepared to pay the price?

We are obviously discussing *subjective* issues here. A PHC practitioner must be willing to satisfy a client's expectations of contact, information, and aesthetics. Just bear in mind that your *personnel must be capable of determining a client's expectations and be prepared to define them on an individual basis.* Your pricing for individual programs (discussed in Chapter 6) will depend upon a thorough understanding of individual client expectations.

... personnel must be capable of determining a client's expectations and be prepared to define them on an individual basis.

CHAPTER SUMMARY

- The decision to implement a Plant Health Care service should be based on a company's short- and long-term goals and careful consideration of current issues and trends within the green industry.
- Because PHC is a new concept to most consumers, marketing and selling efforts must focus on both the benefits of those services and the company's ability to deliver those services.
- A concise mission statement clearly states company objectives and philoso-

phies, and must be known to management, staff, and clients alike. The mission statement of a successful service business states clearly that specific beneficial services will be successfully delivered to a specific market through specific means.
- Much of what clients desire (contact, information, aesthetics) is subjective. Determining expectations of individual clients requires a people-oriented tree care professional skilled in the art of listening.

CHAPTER 4

The PHC Marketing Plan

INTRODUCTION

You've established your mission (the objectives) and now a solid marketing plan (the strategy to achieve those objectives) is needed. As no two companies are identical, it is impossible to create a single marketing plan that would be useful to all companies. This chapter addresses the important ingredients that should be included in your plan.

A Marketing Plan is a strategy for determining the target market for your service, detailing that market's needs and then satisfying those needs better than the competition. A good marketing plan will take into account "the bigger picture"— economic, social and demographic trends that could have an impact on your marketing efforts. In this section, we will help you think through: to whom you should sell; what that group most desires; and how Plant Health Care meets those needs. The first step is to establish your marketing strengths, and we can do so by discussing what is called your "marketing culture."

EXAMINING YOUR MARKETING CULTURE

> *"Marketing culture" refers to the underlying beliefs, values, principles and behaviors that serve as the foundation for a marketing system.*

What makes your company what it is today? What are the core values of your company? What attitudes shape your view of the customer? What are your company's strengths and weaknesses? Answer these questions and you have begun the process of identifying your company's culture. The term "culture" refers to the composite makeup of the company as it exists.

Nations develop their own particular culture, as do organizations, groups, families, or any collection of people. Wherever people associate, under whatever guise, beliefs are shared, expectations arise, and prejudices form. Culture springs out of human activities and perceptions. Likewise, every business develops its own unique culture. Technically speaking, a marketing culture refers to the underlying beliefs, values, principles and behaviors that serve as the foundation for a marketing system. Inherent in this definition is the premise that a strong marketing culture will foster marketing effectiveness if properly channeled. Let's discuss this on a more practical level.

Employees share views. They may develop negative associations of the clientele and prefer little customer contact, or just the opposite may occur. One

> *Each company reflects the makeup and the beliefs of its staff.*

company might hire uneducated seasonal employees who have little or no stake in the company welfare, while another might be made up of a core of highly educated, highly dedicated, year-round employees. Each company reflects the makeup and the beliefs of its staff. Developing an intimate understanding of your own company's culture is your first step toward creating an effective marketing plan. A clear understanding of your company's culture will produce marketing themes that play to the strengths of your company.

But how does one make an accurate appraisal of strengths and weaknesses? Consider the questions in figure 4-1 as you seek to identify the strengths and weaknesses of your company. Put them individually to members within your organization. Then share the answers and compare notes on responses. Out of this process the real strengths of your company will emerge.

Once you have established your strengths and weaknesses from a marketing point-of-view, you are ready to capitalize on your strengths by developing a marketing theme to drive your PHC program.

MARKETING CULTURE

ORGANIZATIONAL

- What are the core values in the company?
- What mission statement guides your organization?
- What image does your company attempt/desire to project?
- In your opinion, what are the company's major strengths?

QUALITY

- How do you view the consumer?
- What counts as quality service?
  - What is it?
  - What does it look like?
  - How do you know when you achieve it?
  - When is it important?
  - In your estimate, what is the present quality of services offered to customers/clients?
- Are your employees educationally motivated? Certified?

MARKET FORCES

- Who is the competition?
  - What makes them competition? What makes you different?
- Who is the customer?
  - What do they believe about companies like yours?
  - What values do they hold which impact your company?
- From the consumer's viewpoint, what are the company's primary strengths and weaknesses?
- What is your competitive advantage

Figure 4 - 1. Questions that, when answered, will help identify a company's strengths and weaknesses — leading to an understanding of the company's marketing culture.

CHOOSING A MARKETING THEME

> *Your marketing theme must develop key features or benefits that stand out.*

Once company strengths and values have been determined you are ready to develop a marketing theme that conforms to the shape of a company. One marketing theme, and not more than one, is the rule.

A marketing theme is the overriding idea — the core of a company's identity and the tool with which a company "positions" itself in the marketplace. Developed with respect to the strengths and direction of a company, it will then serve to reinforce those strengths, shaping and molding the attributes of the services that company offers.

To position your Plant Health Care service, you must look at your target market. How do your consumers perceive the industry and how do they differentiate between companies? As we stated earlier, consumers have both negative and positive perceptions and find it difficult to differentiate between companies. There are several ways for you to create that position for your service in clients' minds. Your marketing theme must develop key features or benefits that stand out.

Let's examine some themes developed in the auto industry and see how, through consistency in their messages, they positioned their automobiles. Mercedes Benz is luxury and engineering; Volvo is luxury and safety; Cadillac and Lincoln are luxury and comfort; and BMW is luxury and roadhandling. All are luxury automobiles, all have built their themes around key aspects, and not one manufacturer has ever apologized for the sticker price. The Volkswagen beetle, known as "the bug" in the '50s and '60s, was positioned (by the manufacturer) as "ugly" and "cheap." While seen as ugly and cheap, it held the lionsshare of the import market and even became a status symbol in its day. These

MARKETING THEMES

CATEGORY	EXAMPLE
ENVIRONMENTAL STRESS	(stresses are opportunities)
PLANTS	(health, aesthetics)
PROPERTY	(investment)
PROFESSIONALISM	(certified arborist)
PRACTITIONER	(experience)
SERVICES/PROCEDURES	(scientific, expertise)
VALUES	(environmentally conscious)
CUSTOMER	(social categories)
PROBLEM	(tree quality loss)
KEY ATTRIBUTE	(contact)
AGAINST A CATEGORY	(lawn care)
AGAINST A SPECIFIC COMPETITOR	(?)

Figure 4 - 2. Examples of marketing themes

> *The key to successful marketing is continuity of theme.*

are examples of very successfully *positioning* automobiles.

You must similarly position your PHC services by picking a theme and testing it. See if it fits your company and positions you for success in the marketplace. More than one theme is confusing to consumers and employees alike. Once you establish confidence that the theme works, develop it. Build upon it. Allow it to work for you and differentiate your company from the competition. The key to successful marketing is continuity of theme. After you have identified issues that differentiate your company and the services it offers and you have selected the theme that will have the most impact based on your customer's needs, you must determine how best to communicate that difference to your target market.

DEVELOPING A THEME FOCUS

In the above example, Mercedes Benz decided to focus on one of its key strengths — engineering — by simply taking inventory of its culture. Engineering is what the company had been famous for. Plant care professionals can choose from a number of possible market focuses. Some are specific to the profession. Some are specific to the company. Some are general. Each could be used to successfully position a company in the marketplace. Following are two fictitious examples.

The easiest way to explain the possibilities of theme development is by example. Take, for instance, a business that wanted to position itself as "plant oriented." Call this company "The Care of Plants." Perhaps as a result of examining its culture, this company decided to deemphasize customer relations and to build their image around the theme — All Plants are Unique. Their goal: to offer a broad range of programs and services emphasizing expert individualized attention for plants. Several PHC program features can now parade this theme. For example, the company may offer: (a) standardized plant inventories, (b) plant "check-ups," (c) customized care programs for each plant on a property, (d) plant replacement guarantees for plants under care, (e) consultations before planting, and so forth.

The key is that each of these features places the focus on the plant first. Customers dealing with "The Care of Plants" would develop clear expectations when dealing with the company. Certain kinds of consumers would find the concept attractive while other kinds might be turned off by the deemphasis on personal attention. The overall appeal of any theme sets the boundaries of a campaign's success.

Take a second example of a specific market focus—the theme of Value. Call the company "Tree Health Inc." Their focus and their slogan are one in the same—"Environmentally Safe Plant Care." Such a company might provide a bevy of features that highlight this theme: (a) a guarantee to check with neighbors before treatments, (b) biorational pest control applications only, (c) an environmental safety report after each contact, (d) perhaps a zero pesticide option. Once again, the theme dictates the key attributes of the PHC program.

Consumers with overriding environmental concerns will come to know and trust that "Tree Health Inc." provides a service that is consistent with their beliefs and values. The company's actions and their advertising gives them every confidence that such a service will continue unabated.

Select a theme that will capitalize on your existing strengths, one that you and your employees can grow with. The key is to develop one theme consistently throughout your program design and marketing efforts. More than one theme will confuse your clients and dilute your strengths. A powerful theme, soundly orchestrated, will attract clients with similar interests.

BRANDING YOUR PHC SERVICE

> *Branding refers to the strategies that distinguish one company's service from another.*

Branding refers to the strategies that distinguish one company's service from another. This can be done, in part, by the name and image you choose for your service. If a new name is to be involved for the company or the new PHC service, now is the time to do it. Once you have chosen a position for your service, you should create a name or brand for the program that will help your target market differentiate that service from others in the marketplace. Branding can also create loyalty with customers. Good branding should build your company's image by quickly conveying the type and quality of your services to your markets. Before you start trying to think of names, make sure you are quite certain of your positioning strategies. The name must reflect your positioning of the service. It should be something that people can easily remember and produces a positive connotation. The name should suggest something about the service's benefits and it should be distinctive. Choosing a good name to brand your service will set your company's service apart.

Once you have settled on a name, you can brand your employees by having them engage in activities consistent with the desired image. Uniforms are perhaps the most obvious form of employee branding, but others are equally prevalent, including the frequency and quality of contact between field arborists and the client, the type of information imparted to the client, and general appearance of the crew and the equipment they use.

A good example of successful branding is United Parcel Service (UPS). When we see that very identifiable brown truck or van, with gold lettering, even at a distance, we know it is UPS. When the delivery person appears at our door or in our office, we instantly recognize the UPS uniform and manner. Almost without exception, transactions with UPS personnel are cordial and businesslike. You always have a way of knowing they have to finish the transaction with you quickly because they have other timely deliveries to make. You get the distinct impression that these people have a clear mission they are fulfilling. The mission is clearly service. All of this is branding — through uniformity, training and focus on mission.

> *Successful PHC branding strategies must communicate the larger vision of PHC — the benefits of long-term, preventive actions.*

Successful PHC branding strategies must communicate the larger vision of PHC — the benefits of long-term, preventive actions. Each employee must have a clear-cut mission. Consider the old story about stonemasons. "What are you doing?" asks a stranger to the first mason. "I'm laying stones," is the reply. "What are you doing?" the second mason is asked. "I'm building a cathedral," he responds. Whereas the first mason has a job, the second mason has a vision. PHC is about having vision for the landscape. Marketing PHC is implementing that vision, about building cathedrals, or more appropriately, landscapes. How many arborists believe that when they prune a tree or apply a horticultural oil they are first and foremost beautifying a property, erecting a landscape? When you can state proudly that arborists on your team both conceive of what they do as PHC and communicate this approach to clients, then brand identity is ensured.

MARKET SEGMENTATION

Look at the total potential market for your services and segment it into groups, based on shared common characteristics. The more specific you are, the more helpful it will be later. The divisions can be based on the type of services that the customers would require and their geographical location. Are they private residential homeowners, property managers, or commercial/industrial? Are they located in Town X, Town Y, or Z county? You can divide the homeowners based on age, the value of their home, the size of their property, approximate income level, number of trees in their yard, etc. Once you have segmented the market, you must determine which group or groups would be most beneficial to target.

TARGET MARKETING

> *Your primary target market will consist of larger transactions with fewer buyers.*
>
> —
>
> *Your secondary target market will consist of smaller transactions with more buyers.*

By targeting specific markets you will get the most value for your marketing efforts. As we have mentioned before, the plant care consumer forms a relatively small subset of the overall population. You must differentiate between groups and target the group that has the most potential for your service. That main consuming group will be your primary target market.

Your primary target market (fewer buyers, larger transactions) should be the core focus of your attention and it should represent over 50% of your business. If it is much less, you should consider broadening your criteria. You must also make sure that this market will be large enough to sustain growth for your company. The better you know your primary target market, the better you will be able to market to them. An example of a primary target market could be property owners that have over ten trees on their property, are over 40 years old and have an annual income over $50,000. If that target market is too large to work with, then narrow it down to a sub-segment, like those with incomes in excess of $80,000.

Remember that our research has found that almost half of the customers were college educated and over half had an income in excess of $50,000. Over 70 percent were over 40 years old and had lived in their home for over 5 years. Most customers owned their property and had over 10 trees. This gives you a general idea of where to start searching for a target market. You may get a good deal of mileage by swapping notes with other professionals who have access to clients in your primary market, such as architects, landscape architects, pool builders, house builders, interior designers, and home remodelers.

Now define your secondary target markets (more buyers, smaller transactions), which can be made up of consumers in a group that represent a smaller percentage of the volume, but contain a higher level of purchasers. If you have to broaden the criteria of your primary market so that it encompasses at least 50% of your customer base, it can create a diluting effect on your potential market. If that happens, create several secondary target markets that better describe the smaller groups in your primary market. Be sure not to overlook non-traditional consumers, such as property managers, golf course and park superintendents, and real estate developers. Once you have determined to whom you are going to sell, you can begin to look closely at how Plant Health Care meets those needs.

THE COMPETITION

Now consider your competition. Who are your major competitors? How are those companies different from yours? How are they marketing their services and to whom? Are they using advertising, direct mail or promotions? How successful are their efforts? What are their strengths and weaknesses, and what are their objectives? It is necessary to know what your competitor is doing so

> *... know what your competitor is doing.*

that you can plan accordingly. In looking at the competition, do not limit your search to tree care companies that are performing the same type of services that your company does. Make sure to consider companies such as nurseries and other landscape companies that provide consulting services. Good competition can be healthy for your business and keep your company "on its toes." In a broader sense, keen competition can generally raise consumer awareness of your industry's services.

MARKETING OBJECTIVES

> *Marketing objectives are the cornerstone of your marketing plan.*

Marketing objectives are the cornerstone of your marketing plan. They dictate what needs to be done to reach your sales goals and must be quantifiable and measurable. They must focus on influencing the behavior of the target market. Your objective could be to retain your present clients or to increase their level of business. It could also be to attract new clients. To develop your marketing objectives, you begin by reviewing your sales objectives and why you set them at a certain level. For example, if you determined that your sales objective would be to increase sales by 10%, your marketing objective could be to increase the amount each client is spending with your company by 5% and the additional 5% would come from new clients.

Your marketing objectives should incorporate broad trends that could provide opportunities for, but not pose threats to, your business. Are there demographic factors that could have an impact on your business? Are people and companies moving in or out of your area? Are new homes being built and are they upscale? These factors can be very important, especially if they are changes that are taking place in your target markets. What are the trends in the environment? Although individual property owners may not be concerned about the use of pesticides on their properties, governmental agencies are moving toward increased regulation. Plant Health Care is a proactive response to this governmental trend. By solving problems or exploiting opportunities you are able to determine your objectives. What are your short term objectives? What are your long term objectives?

SALES OBJECTIVES

Sales objectives are the realistic monetary goals you set for your company. They give your plan (and sales team) direction and must be challenging, but attainable. The objectives must be measurable in terms of dollars sold and customers serviced. Both, dollars and customers should increase. Base sales objectives on previous performance. If there are plans for across-the-board increases in your rates, plug them in when looking at the previous year's sales. Obviously, a 10% increase in prices will appear to be a 10% increase in sales. Any increases must be factored in before new objectives are set. What are your sales objectives for the short term (one year or less?) What are your sales objectives for the long term (three years or more?)

MARKETING MIX

The marketing mix consists of variable internal activities that you can control — those activities that allow you to set the stage for creating your image and selling your services. What do you want to tell your target audience? What mix of services will you offer? Will your pricing structure look more like Kmart or Neiman Marcus? Many of the items listed in figure 4-3 are self-explanatory. Services offered, pricing strategies and methods of selling will vary from company to company and these activities require individualized consideration and decisions.

The promotional strategies you use should reinforce the positioning of your service and create a unified image around your marketing theme. The theme is your strongest claim, one that is linked to the unique aspects or features of your service. Promotions should have a similar look, sound or tone. This way they will build on each other for the maximum effect. Where will you choose to communicate this message? Will you advertise in the phone book, the local paper or trade papers that target specific segments of your target market? Will you prepare spots for radio or cable television? Answers to these questions depend upon the other elements of the plan.

You have defined your target market and you know what they desire. You have chosen a position for your service and have developed branding strategies. Now you are ready to convey your message in a way that will get the customer's attention, hold their interest, build their awareness, arouse their desire and get them to act? There are four major tools that can be used to promote your business: advertising, sales promotion, public relations, and selling strategies. For the benefit of the many companies that have not previously been involved in significant promotional activities, we offer the following.

ADVERTISING

Many of your advertising decisions will be based on your existing image. If you have a well-known positive image in your market area, you can afford to do less promotion because you can place less emphasis on your standards, dependability, and overall professionalism. These qualities can be subtly built into advertising revolving around your theme and positioning statements. If you are introducing new services, seeking significant expansion and are less well known, you may do well to mix generic company promotion talking up these attributes with service-specific promotion. Let's look at two examples which demonstrate the point.

If Maytag were to introduce a line of appliances which they had not previously marketed, the bulk of their advertising messages could be product-specific needing only a tag line at the end of a commercial to remind us that they are the "dependability people." If a company which we had never heard of introduces a new quality line of the same appliance, they would need a much larger budget because they would have to establish their credibility with regard to quality standards as well as selling the benefits and features of their new line. In recent years, Lexus appeared on the market with a line of cars we had never heard of. Initially, their promotional activities sold luxury and quality (the company). They've made their point and today their advertising can be model-specific and simply elude to Lexus' quality.

How will you get word out to prospective PHC clients? Knocking on doors (cold calls) is one way, but is extremely labor intensive. There are many promotional avenues which can produce qualified leads before the sales call — some are better than others. You may do well to consider mixing the activities listed below. We have omitted television and phone solicitations. While both are available, television advertising is typically not cost effective in most areas, and telephone solicitations are often regarded as "intrusions" and can turn off many potential prospects.

> *The promotional strategies you use should reinforce the positioning of your service and create a unified image around your marketing theme.*

> *There are many promotional avenues which can produce qualified leads before the sales call.*

> *The marketing mix consists of variable internal activities that you can control.*

MARKETING MIX

SERVICES
- Image
- Packages, families
- Product quality
- Safety
- Aesthetics
- Tree/landscape health
- Problem eradication/prevention
- Process quality
- Pleasantness
- Accessibility
- Responsiveness

PRICE
- Price levels
- Payment terms
- Seasonal discounts
- Frequency discounts
- Quantity discounts
- Incentives
- Guarantees

SELLING
- Sales paths
- Service support
- Message strategies

PROMOTION
- Themes/continuity
- Publicity
- Advertising/Direct contact messages
- Special Events
- Promotional Items
- Samplings

Figure 4 - 3. The PHC marketing mix consisting of variable, controlable activities.

Direct Mail is possibly the most productive for landscape services and highly recommended. It allows you to zero in on your target market. Unlike any other medium, your promotional materials are available to review when the prospect has the time to read them. Securing a mailing list is the only drawback to this option. It is difficult to purchase an appropriate list because of the characteristics of the prospect and small geographic areas involved. Residential lists of a specific zip code are generally available but will include addresses of unlikely buyers. Scouting neighborhoods and securing addresses may be the best option in some areas.

Newspaper ads placed in the home, garden, or financial sections will be seen by many prospects and if compelled to act, can work well. This medium is good for generating leads and especially good for creating a lasting image even if the prospect isn't ready to buy. One disadvantage is the fact that few people will cut out your ad before recycling the newspaper. Some newspapers deliver advertising supplements (inserts) to specific areas of the community.

Yellow page advertising that shouts quality and professionalism works well for general landscape services. PHC, however, is a service that requires more selling than could probably be accomplished in a yellow page ad. It is commonplace for people to develop a positive feeling for a company through other media even though they aren't yet ready to buy. If you're doing other things right to gain name recognition, when buying time comes, prospects will look no further than your ad or line listing.

Radio is an alternative in some areas. If your locale has a few major radio stations, then this medium becomes more attractive. If your market is in Los Angeles, for example, with over 250 stations to choose from, then just selecting the station to reach your prospect could become a life's work. Should you have a popular easy listening station that features news and information during morning and evening drive time, it could be excellent for reaching your target audience. All stations have audience statistics they will be eager to share. Radio stations will more often than not be able to help you with production of your spots for a reasonable or no charge.

OTHER PROMOTIONAL ACTIVITIES

Special events — Here again, every locale is different. If your area has garden and/or home shows, it might be worth your while to set up a booth. The booth and signage can be costly, but properly done, can be an excellent investment.

Talk Radio — Having a regular Saturday morning radio show during the growing season could be excellent. If you and/or a staff member have the necessary skills, the format could be informative dialog specific to your locale with or without a "call in" segment. It could also be sponsorship of a "canned" or syndicated program relating to landscaping or gardening.

Networking — Get active. For example, membership in service clubs such as Kiwanis, Lions, Rotary or Exchange are excellent opportunities for meeting prospects. The local chamber of commerce and economic development council are likely to have active participants who could use your services. These activities take time but are usually well worth it.

Conduct Classes — Hold educational classes on tree and other landscape care in a local community education program or at your place of business.

Promotional items — An item which you can leave with a prospect after an initial sales call or something you give to active customers always promotes good feelings about your company. Looking in the yellow pages under "Advertising specialties" can usually direct you to a company that sells thousands of specialty items in various price ranges. Whatever item you choose, make it classy!

PUBLICITY

The International Society of Arboriculture has a PHC-specific press package available for your use. It is basically feature article material that you can take to the home/garden editor of your local newspaper and sit down and discuss. By developing a rapport with the editor and explaining the benefits (especially reduced chemical reliance - environmental aspects) of PHC, it is likely that you can end up with some favorable press. Also, it is beneficial to make PHC brochures available to local garden clubs and even provide a speaker for one of their meetings.

PRODUCTION

One of the biggest obstacles you may have to overcome after deciding what media to use for promotional activities, is finding production help. You have to decide what you want to say to build on your marketing theme. You have to determine how to say it so as to generate a positive image. As we stated, radio stations will generally provide assistance in generating radio spots, but what about print media. A lot depends on *where* you are. Here are some things to consider.

Advertising agencies are available, but are they for you? You may encounter everything from large full service agencies to the boutique variety. Either way, they typically seek accounts that allow them to supply a variety of services and shy away from job work. Unless you have a large advertising budget, your business probably won't be attractive to agencies.

So are you out of luck? No. In the age of desktop publishing, there are freelancers everywhere; finding the good ones is the problem. There are probably some very capable freelance designers and typesetters within your area. They are often home-based with low overhead and may have a good business going through word-of-mouth referrals. Some of the best may not be listed in the yellow pages. You can check with local printers, typesetting service bureaus, and other advertisers that you suspect don't have an agency to find these people. They can prepare professional layouts and they may know of good copy professionals to aid in final copywriting. These people will generally be glad to meet you in your office. Look at samples of their work and discuss their pricing structures. It may take some time, but keep looking until you find the people that are right for you — your image is worth the effort.

> *You have to decide what you want to say to build on your marketing theme. You have to determine how to say it so as to generate a positive image.*

THE PHC MARKETING PLAN

We have now covered everything you need to craft the plan itself. Figure 4-4 provides an outline of the issues and questions relevant to this task. Overall, your task is to establish financial and marketing goals and design a marketing strategy to meet those objectives. That marketing strategy will involve creating a position in the mind of the customer for your Plant Health Care service. It will also involve naming or branding the service and packaging it in such a way as to differentiate it from what is offered by other companies. You will need to establish budgets for capital expenditures which could include a new computer system, vehicles, equipment, uniforms, etc. Your plan should factor in any additional personnel and training which will be required. You will also need to decide which advertising/sales promotion media would be most effective for promoting your service and establish budgets for these activities.

To those already dreding the task at hand, let us leave you with one last thought. If your company has been around for a few years, is showing profits, and has a loyal client base, then you already possess marketing expertise, regardless of how formally you have employed it. The business environment is becoming increasingly sophistocated, however, and it may be time for formal planning rather than operating on "gut feelings."

The marketing plan worksheet on the following page will guide you through the relevant issues to craft your plan.

> *If your company has been around for a few years, then you've already been doing some good marketing.*

MARKETING PLAN WORKSHEET

PART I

- Describe Your PHC Service
- Major Service Attributes *(list at least 5)*
- Major Marketing Theme (investment, reflected aesthetics, etc.)
- Describe your Primary Target Market (decision-makers, demographic profile, beliefs about service)
- Describe your Secondary Target Market (decision-makers, demographic profile, beliefs about service)

PART II

- Short-Term Objectives
- Rationale
- Long-Term Objectives
- Rationale
- Branding Strategies *(list at least 4)*
- Promotional Strategies *(list at least 4)*

PART III

- Selling Strategies *(list as many as possible)*
- Pricing Strategies *(list as many as possible)*

PART IV

- Estimate the Average Price for Service
- Estimate the Average Price per Customer per Year
- Sales Projection: Number of Customers Using Service per Year
- Estimate Primary Short-term (1-year) Costs of Providing Service per Customer:
  A. Labor
  B. Supplies
  C. Direct Cost of Sales
  D. Miscellaneous
- Estimate Primary Long-Term (3-year) Costs
  A. Equipment Budget
  B. Training Budget
  C. Promotion Budget
  D. Miscellaneous
- Short-Term Sales Objectives: Necessary Customers
- Short-Term Sales Goal
- Long-Term Sales Objectives: Necessary Customers
- Long-Term Sales Goal

Figure 4-4. Outline of the issues and questions relevant to development of the marketing plan.

CHAPTER SUMMARY

- A Plant Health Care marketing plan is a strategy for determining to whom you should sell (the target market), what that group most desires (market's needs), how PHC meets those needs, and then satisfying those needs better than the competition.
- Identifying your marketing culture is the first step in developing a marketing plan. Once company strengths and values have been determined, marketing themes can be designed. The key to successful marketing is the selection of a theme that capitalizes on your strengths and then sticking with it.
- Recognize marketing goals and design a marketing strategy based on those goals. Remember:
  — target marketing results in more value for your effort
  — marketing objectives are the cornerstone of a marketing plan
  — positioning and branding will separate you from the competition
  — select promotion strategies that reinforce your marketing theme.

CHAPTER 5

PHC Marketing: Selling the Service

INTRODUCTION

After examining your business, setting goals and targeting the potential client, the business of initiating contacts and building relationships begins. With Plant Health Care this means that every step of the process should be directed toward giving the customer what they most desire: *Contact, Information* and *Aesthetics*.

Traditionally, landscape companies had to realize two goals in a marketing effort. First, marketing had to attract customers to the company, through image enhancement and/or messages designed to address specific client needs. (An example of this might be an ad offering pruning at a discount.) Second, and more importantly, the marketing effort had to result in a contract for services. For many services, this has been accomplished through house-to-house calls, responding to inquiries and estimates through referrals. Plant Health Care, must take a different approach.

Plant Health Care is a contact-intensive undertaking. Beginning with the sales effort and proceeding to client relations, every point in the process depends upon initiating, developing and maintaining personal a working relationship with the client. A face-to-face on-site landscape evaluation is the Target Behavior of PHC marketing. Contracts for work are a direct result of successfully achieving this target behavior. Marketing efforts that emphasize the contract over the on-site contact miss the mark.

A PHC marketing campaign must engage its audience immediately. The marketing message must be considered as the opening line of a conversation — the first words of what will be a long-term relationship. These words should speak directly to a client's needs in such a way that the client has a desire to know more, to continue the conversation.

> *Plant Health Care is a contact intensive undertaking.*

CUSTOMIZED PROMOTIONAL MATERIALS

INFORMATION BROCHURE PROMOTION

Personal contact is the emphasis of this approach as salespeople are encouraged to hand-deliver this promotion whenever possible — or to leave it in a doorway or a mailbox as a last resort. Beyond establishing personal contact, the main idea of the promotion is to provide clients with "*some timely information*" regarding one of the plants on their property. This information can take the form of a brochure or an informational sheet such as those published by state agricultural agencies or the agricultural departments of colleges and universities. Landscape care companies have access to a large array of materials that would provide consumers with information of great interest.

The PHC Compendium is an excellent resource bibliography. Many other brochures and pamphlets cross your desk on a regular basis and cover a wide variety of subjects pertaining to plant care. Frequently available for little or no cost to the arborist, these informational pieces are potentially powerful marketing tools.

Remember that consumers value information. Take stock of the large array of materials in your files that would be of particular interest to the clients you have chosen to target. By choosing carefully from among the host of inexpensive brochures and informational plant care pamphlets at your disposal it is possible to find materials which will fit a large variety of situations in the field. By matching informational brochures to specific properties, you make a statement of great impact and create the immediate impression of being a company dedicated to high levels of personal service. By developing innovative and unique ways of placing information in the hands of potential clients, you assure that your messages will receive consideration.

Implementation of the specified design, illustrated in Figure 5-1, will assure a tasteful and intriguing end product. The optional message serves the same function. All in all this promotion is intended to cast a company as forward thinking, responsible, and dependable. If the enclosed brochure is indeed timely, this approach can and will hit the mark.

TREE VALUATION PROMOTION

Information and contact drive this promotion as well. The information provided, however, responds to the financial concerns of property owners. Having identified and targeted a prospective client, the salesperson/appraiser assesses the value of the client's landscape from a roadside observation point. Utilizing a custom template, the salesperson creates an impressive and customized APPRAISAL OF TREE VALUES for the specific property (Figs. 5-2a, b, c). This appraisal, along with the persuasive letter will then be sent as a package to the homeowner. Again, a precise implementation of this design, illustrated in the next few pages, will ensure the effectiveness of the promotion.

Together, these materials combine to offer homeowners compelling reasons to further investigate the benefits of Plant Health Care.

DEVELOPING A PHC SALES PATH

Once you obtain an appointment for a landscape evaluation with the prospective client, you must formulate your sales path for the meeting. A sales path is a common pattern or approach that one follows on a sales call. It can be seen as a series of logical statements that build, one upon the other, as a salesperson attempts to persuade. Or the arguments can cut across logic and into emotional terrain to operate on the levels of value and belief. Either way, the desired result is persuasion.

Historically the tree care profession has tried to sell safety, the health and vigor of trees and aesthetics, in that order. The reasoning is sound enough in one sense. The argument for safety is relatively unimpeachable and the expertise of the salesperson will tend to reinforce the claim. The desired result is a

INFORMATION BROCHURE CAMPAIGN

CONCEPT: To use existing information brochures consistent with your company's image to introduce the company to prospective clients.

AUDIENCE: Prospective clients.

GIVE-AWAY: Tree care brochures and fact sheets

DISTRIBUTION: Hand-delivered when possible; otherwise placed near house entryway.

THE ENVELOPE

Front: Business size, large enough for the brochure. Opening at the side rather than behind. Grey. A weighted paper with texture. A border runs across the bottom front of the envelope, in the company color. The company name is in the top left hand corner of the envelope.

The envelope is always hand addressed (for example, Mr. Smith) and should follow with:
"Some Timely Information on Dogwood Anthracnose Enclosed" or similar message appropriate for the brochure used. Always *"Some timely information..."*

Back: If possible, the envelope is secured using the string and circle closure common to inter-office business envelopes. The flap is somewhat larger than normal.

A pen and ink drawing of a tree sits centered on the closure, proportionate, leaving say a 3/16" border at the top and at the bottom of the flap. A red, red apple has fallen from the tree. To the ground, where it sits.

Open the envelope.

There is the apple, in the identical place as on the envelope. In small print:
"Some fruit from the tree of knowledge".
Courtesy of [company name].

INSIDE

1. Brochure
2. An insert of stiff paper, the same as the envelope, with a border of the same color as the strip across the front of the envelope.

MESSAGE

- You appreciate personal service.
- Results, not excuses, impress you.
- You want a company that can meet your tree care needs. Possibly the full range of your landscape needs as well.
- Progressive. Expert. Educated. Dependable.
- You've just described [company name].
- We'll let you know what those other companies have yet to discover.

[phone number]

[company name]

Figure 5 - 1. Example of a well-planned information brochure campaign.

42 / THE PLANT HEALTH CARE MANAGEMENT SYSTEM

TREE VALUATION PROMOTION

CONCEPT: To illustrate the large investment homeowners possess in trees

AUDIENCE: High-income, prospective customers

GIVE-AWAY: Abbreviated tree valuation assessment

DISTRIBUTION: First Class Mail

DESIGN: We envision a simple presentation folder mailed in a white 10" x 13" envelope. The address label should be typed and centered on the envelope, and a sticker or stamp should offer the following message:

ENCLOSED ARE TREE VALUES
FOR YOUR PROPERTY

Inside the folder. In the left pocket the reader will find of a persuasive letter which attempts to invoke a strong image. In the right pocket will sit a one-page tree appraisal, similar to the design below. This format for this appraisal should be printed on a white heavy text stock.

Illustrating the appraisal. We recommend that the company invest in a custom form to be made by a local typesetting/imaging service. We suggest dry-transfer images by Letraset for illustrating plantings.

Figure 5 - 2 (a). Description and specifications of a tree valuation promotion.

[company logo]

RE: Front Grounds, 2764 Chestnut Hill Road
Date: August 15, 1992
Field Representative: Bill Smith

[site and plantings illustrated here]

Total Tree Values of Planting Identified: $ _____

Appraiser: _____

This appraisal was made at roadside by a certified arborist of the [name] Company and represents only a partial estimate of the overall value of the property's plantings. These figures are rough estimates and must not be used for insurance or legal purposes.

Figure 5 - 2 (b). Example of an appraisal form to used in a tree valuation promotion. Actual form should be 8 1/2" x 11".

Message on Company letterhead

[date]

Dear Homeowner,

Who can place a value on a tree?

— A tree that guards the foot of a drive, shading the way, inviting and welcoming those who pass beneath.

— A tree that stands astride a lawn, great and colossal, conferring shade and beauty and a sense of place?

Who can estimate the worth of the visual centerpiece of a landscape? The hundred-year-old oak? The magnificent beech that holds the children's swing with its massive arms?

We can.

We are [company name], a full service landscape maintenance company. For the past [number] years, homeowners, businesses and companies in the [local name] area have depended upon us to make the tough judgements and decisions about trees and shrubs and lawns. Decisions requiring expertise and experience.

Keep a tree or take it down? Cable? Treat a diseased plant or let it fend for itself because the expense would be unjustified? Aesthetic concerns do battle with the financial bottom line.

And yet what we've noticed again and again is how little preventive care it takes to keep most of a property owner's horticultural troubles at bay.

An ounce of prevention if you will.

Take a minute to look at the sample tree value appraisal enclosed in your folder, keeping in mind that only a portion of your property has been appraised.

Generally speaking, we find that most people are unaware of the real value of their plantings. The numbers shock.

But there are others who simply nod, understanding that they paid a large sum of money for both house and grounds. These are the people who understand that their landscape is part of a very large investment.

AN INVESTMENT.

Trees, shrubs, lawns. Each, in turn, affects the way in which a property is valued or assessed by the market place.

A tree can be an asset. Or a liability. Depending upon the care it receives or the neglect that it suffers, the return rises or falls.

Well-maintained plantings strengthen property values at the very same time that they provide pleasure and delight for the property owner.

Look out the window and consider your landscape, rich with uncommonly unique potential.

What other investment can be looked on and enjoyed? Climbed on or frolicked over? Growing in size and value.

What other investment pays such handsome dividends in the here and now, as well as over time?

We have found that small amounts of care pay big dividends.

In the next several days you will receive an invitation to contact a representative of [company name] to discuss the ways in which you can protect and maintain your landscape investment.

Think of it this way: You have an opportunity to get in on the ground floor of something big.

Sincerely,

Figure 5 - 2 (C). Possible content for a form letter to accompany a tree appraisal in the tree valuation promotion.

contract for pruning and a foot in the door. Beyond safety, the traditional sales call argues for maintaining a plant's health and vigor, by offering fertilization programs and the like. The argument follows that an increase in aesthetics will result. Still, the overriding perception will remain that the arborist's main concern is safety and that tree health and aesthetics are merely by-products of these concerns. The traditional sales call casts the arborist as a tree-pruning service first, and as a tree maintenance service second with the focus always remaining on safety. The Plant Health Care sales path is different.

Traditional Sales Path
- Safety
- Health and Vigor of Trees
- Aesthetics

Plant Health Care Sales Path
- Building Rapport
- Clarifying Holistic Approach
- Establishing Client Expectations
- Sharing Information
- Exploring PHC Contact
- Promise of Aesthetics

> *The goal of the PHC Sales Path is to establish a long-term relationship with the homeowner.*

The goal of the PHC Sales Path is to establish a long-term relationship with the homeowner. This relationship, more than any particular product or service, is what is being sold. The PHC sales path involves 6 steps, beginning with the concept of PHC.

1. Building Rapport. The focus of your efforts at the beginning of the appointment is to establish enough credibility and rapport so that you can ask all the questions you need to. People buy from people they like. In building a rapport, you try to find a common ground to build from. It could be a conversation about children, because you noticed some toys in the yard or just an appreciation for healthy plants and trees. The conversation helps you to get to know each other better. It is a balancing act, though. You must be aware of the customer's time constraints and follow the pace they set. Building rapport is an ongoing effort throughout the appointment, so continue this effort as you move toward the second step.

2. Clarifying the PHC Approach. The salesperson begins the sales conversation by describing an approach to plants that focuses first and foremost on the benefits of plant health. Pests are described as manifestations of imbalances or unfavorable conditions. Plant Health Care is described as the ongoing process of creating and maintaining plant health. In effect, the discussion of the holistic approach of PHC is meant as an argument for the benefits that accrue from establishing an on-going, long-term relationship with the arborist. Instead of casting the arborist as a mechanic, on-property to merely "fix" a plant and leave, this approach is meant to style the arborist as a trusted care-taker.

PHC addresses the clients need for peace of mind. Comparing PHC to preventive medicine will give clients a hook to hang their understanding on. Health and vigor are the best defense against problems, providing insurance against decline and disaster. PHC is plant management and not pest management. When pests occur, the Plant Health Care strategy could best be summarized as pest suppression rather than pest eradication. While many people believe that all insects are harmful or destructive, the truth of the matter is that relatively few insects will damage plants. Use this point to justify the holistic approach.

Explain that plant health is the first line of defense in a PHC program. By establishing health first, PHC takes a proactive posture against pests.

KEY DIALOGUE

Plant Health Care is simple to understand. Plants, like humans, grow best when all of their needs are met. So, if you create healthy plants, if you create the conditions for best health and keep the systems of a plant in balance, then the natural defenses of a plant will tend to protect that plant from pests and diseases. Doing that, you not only get a plant that is more resistant to pests and diseases, you get a plant that is bursting with vitality.

Plant Health Care is environmentally-sensitive plant management. Focused on plant health rather than pest eradication, PHC is socially responsible plant care. Yet while PHC is soft on the environment it is hard on pests.

3. **Establishing Client Expectations.** The second step along the sales path places the focus on the client, as the salesperson asks a range of detailed questions meant to uncover the range of the client's expectations. Plant Health Care is every bit as sensitive and responsive to the needs of the client as it is to the needs of plants. Without a clear understanding of client expectations, and without the framework for on-going communication, the client/arborist relationship can short-circuit in any one of a thousand ways. Favorite plants, expectations of cost, aesthetic considerations, feelings about insect and disease presence—all of these must be taken into consideration. By becoming aware of client beliefs, a practitioner can hope to modify them and bring them in line with the right notions of PHC. The customer's expectations must be understood and respected. Without this, there is no relationship at all.

It is tempting to start an appointment with the customer by listing all of the services that you can offer and explaining the benefits of Plant Health Care. You must suppress this temptation. They will want to know the cost right away. As you mention each service they will be thinking that it is getting more and more expensive. So you then find yourself telling them the price before you have been able to relate the value of the services. You must strategically create that value through questioning. That is not to say that you withhold information that they desire. On the contrary, you are there to provide them with information based on your knowledge and experience.

Your goal is to gather the necessary background information on the specific problem the customer wants to address and try to uncover other areas of concern. By asking strategic questions, you can guide the client away from just thinking about the one problem that they called you about, and thinking more about their whole yard. It is important to find out what aspect of this customer's landscape has the most emotional value. Do they have trees or plants on their property that possibly were planted to commemorate a family event, a row of hemlocks that ensures privacy for their backyard or a stately oak that frames the house?

One question type, commonly called **Situation Questions**, help you to discover customer expectations. In essence, these are fact-finding questions.

SAMPLE SITUATION QUESTION DIALOGUE
"Which trees and plants are you most concerned with?"
"Have these [fruit] trees been treated lately?"
"You mentioned a [holly] your father gave you for an anniversary present last year, where is it?"
"How often do you water those shrubs?"

Situation questions help you to discover customer expectations.

"That's a beautiful [oak] tree, when was that cement patio built around it?"

"I noticed some toys by the garage and a dog house. You have small children and pets?"

"Did you plant those [maples] on the side of your lawn under those telephone wires or were they there when you moved in?"

"Are those your shrubs at the edge of the property on that side? Where does your property line end on the other side of your yard? Is privacy important for you?"

---

4. Sharing of Information. Research shows that plant care clientele clearly desire information about the trees and shrubs on their property. Recognizing this, your next step in the sales path is to walk the property, identify key plants and provide the property owner with information regarding these plants. The key is to provide this information through a question format, rather than a show and tell format. Questions place the focus on the consumer and maintain interest.

Three question types are of great importance in this step. Many of your situation questions in the previous step can now be followed with **Problem Questions**. Arborists lean toward this type of question naturally because of the investigative nature of PHC. Problem questions try to uncover areas of dissatisfaction for the client.

> *Problem questions try to uncover areas of dissatisfaction for the customer.*

SAMPLE PROBLEM QUESTION DIALOGUE

"You have been personally spraying your fruit trees twice a year, how has that worked out?"

"How long have you had a problem with your [holly]?"

"Are you having problems with the shrubs on the south side of your house?"

"Have you started to have a lot more dead branches on that big [oak] lately?"

"How do you feel about the use of pesticides?"

"Those [maples] usually grow pretty high, do you think you might have a problem with the wires?"

"You mentioned that more than privacy, you are most concerned with your neighbor's ugly tool shed?"

The next type of question is the **Suggestive Question**. These questions are best integrated along with the problem questions, flowing naturally after key points. They suggest implications of the problems and verify that they are important to the client.

> *Suggestive questions suggest implications of the problems and verify that they are important to the client.*

SAMPLE SUGGESTIVE QUESTION DIALOGUE

"So, your [fruit] trees really aren't growing the way that you would like them too, even though you have been spraying them?"

"So, the pests in your [holly bush] come back every year?"

"You have been watering those shrubs often, but the leaves are still turning brown?"

"Do you ever worry about some of those big dead branches from that [oak] tree hanging over your children's bedroom? I'm surprised the branches weathered that storm we had last November."

"Now you mentioned that you aren't really happy with using a lot of pesticides, especially with your kids playing outside in the yard so much?"

"Unless those wires are moved, those maples are going to eventually have to be cut back so they don't interfere, aren't they? But you really want some shade on *that part of the yard though, right?"*

"So you have thought of planting something on that side of your yard to cover up that tool shed, but you aren't sure what would create the best screen?"

> **Solution questions get the client involved by focusing on solutions.**

Solution Questions are the last type of questions. They take the suggestive questions a step further. Rather than dredge up all the problems and implied needs and just leave them there, creating what can be a negative atmosphere, they get the client involved by focusing on solutions. Here you can repeat the benefits of a long-term, holistic approach.

SAMPLE SOLUTION QUESTION DIALOGUE

"Well, spraying isn't always the answer. Would you like me to take a closer look at it to see what the problem is?

"Can I take a quick look at that [holly]. You know I have some information about [holly] in my truck, would you like to have a copy?"

"Here, take a look, see the roots around the base of these shrubs...?"

"Maybe a couple of those dead branches should be taken down on that [oak], before they cause some real damage?"

"With the children playing in the yard so much, you might want to reduce the need for pesticides?"

"The maples are still young, maybe they should be moved to another part of the yard where their growth would be uninhibited? And since you really want some shade on that side of the yard, we might want to talk about some trees that don't grow too high and wouldn't interfere with the wires?"

"So it would be helpful to have some suggestions as to what would make the best natural screen for that tool shed?"

Taken out of context these questions might seem too obvious, but filtered throughout a discussion they can be highly effective. It is important for you to uncover problems and needs, but you are much closer to PHC sales when clients understand what you will do and how you will do it. Use your questions to get clients involved with their property.

You have asked *Situation Questions* to find out all the facts and you have asked *Problem Questions* to uncover areas of dissatisfaction. You have used this information to ask *Suggestive Questions* that help a client to perceive the impact of the problem and *Solution Questions* that create a positive framework for the discussion. Now you can reiterate PHC and how it meets specific needs. You are giving them solutions to their problems and getting them involved, rather than just giving them all the advantages up front about how an integrated plan for the health of their plants and shrubs will save them time and money. *People don't buy advantages — People buy solutions.*

Also keep in mind that research shows that while consumers may not be opposed to the blanket spraying of chemicals on their property they do have a strong aversion to the use of the word spray. Consequently, spray is out and treatments, tactics, and pest control strategies are in.

5. Exploring PHC Contact. Plant Care consumers also value contact. PHC is contact intensive. Monitoring and threshold values are strong selling points of the program. Salespeople should clearly explain the process of inspection and monitoring as well as the benefits this contact provides. PHC provides peace of mind and protection against loss.

6. Promise of Aesthetics. Last but not least is the promise of a beautiful landscape. As the argument for PHC builds, this promise will undoubtedly find its way into the conversation repeatedly. This is a positive argument and with most clients a critical one. A salesperson can promise this as one of the by-

> *Plant Health Care is designed to develop a long-term relationship with the customer.*

products of plant health. Sell PHC as information, contact and aesthetics. Sell yourself and your company by displaying your knowledge, experience and skill with PHC. Remember that your manner and method of questioning will help to establish credibility. Through your questioning you develop the prospective client's desire for solutions. PHC solutions have value.

The Plant Health Care Sales Path is a carefully constructed argument based on consumer research. This path is meant to set the groundwork for a relationship. What is being sold are the attributes of Plant Health Care as well as the attributes of an individual company. Contracts for services follow on the heels of the relationship. Generally speaking, two types of selling/buying situations exist: short term sales and long term relationships. Plant Health Care is designed to develop a long term relationship with the customer. By uncovering needs and problems and helping the client see the importance and implications of those problems, you are creating a situation where the customer desires a solution and you have the answer. But it is an answer that you both have arrived at, rather than one that you just dictated. If the prospective client sees enough value in your service, the closing line can be as simple and appropriate as "When can we start?" No need for tricky techniques to corner the customer. A heavy handed "hard sell" close at the end of a sales call can actually backfire in the long-run.

KEY DIALOGUE

Care programs which simply emphasize pest control can only promise that plants will appear healthy. By actually creating healthy plants, PHC promises vigor, growth, beauty and a reduction in the costs of care over the long term. With increased health and plant growth, PHC actually provides a return on the plant care investment. Long term costs decrease as the value of well-tended plantings soar. PHC is an investment in landscape value. More important, PHC is cost-effective plant management.

By meeting essential needs, PHC creates plants that are healthy and vigorous—a roots-to-crown health that pays dividends in beauty.

PHC VIDEO, SALES AIDS AND COMPENDIUM

A 12-minute video that explains PHC to tree care consumers and sales aids are available from the International Society of Arboriculture and the National Arborist Association. These marketing tools can be used as an introduction or as a follow-up to a PHC client contact. Because of their ability to speak informatively to the needs of consumers at the same time that they persuasively convey the benefits of Plant Health Care, these tools can be relied upon to help set the tone of things to come.

A PHC Compendium listing close to 2000 circulars and bulletins is available to arborists on electronic media. It can be obtained through the International Society of Arboriculture and the National Arborist Association.

CHAPTER SUMMARY

- PHC marketing must engage its audience, thus personal contacts are essential. The target behavior of PHC marketing must be a face-to-face landscape evaluation.

- Informational brochures can be effective promoters of personal contact. Both information and personal contact underpin the suggested tree valuation promotion.
- The 6 steps of the PHC sales path are to:
  — build rapport
  — clarify the PHC approach
  — establish client expectations
  — share information to address problem and solution questions
  — explore PHC contact
  — promise aesthetics.

CHAPTER 6

PHC Marketing: Pricing Programs

INTRODUCTION

Plant Health Care is a new concept to almost every potential client. It is also a new profit center for many tree care companies and many facets of operating a plant health care business may appear unfamiliar. Probably the most difficult business decisions with PHC involve pricing. The most frequent criticism of IPM was that there was only a single "cadillac" approach to managing clients' properties. This "all or nothing" approach limited the client's option to a simple yes or no and probably accounted for low enrollment in many of the early IPM programs. Plant Health Care should offer an array of possibilities for the client. Programs must be created to fit the needs and expectations of the client rather than the other way around. There are two broad approaches to pricing PHC — tree management or landscape management.

TREE MANAGEMENT APPROACH

While Plant Health Care reaches its fullest potential when an entire landscape is managed, it is possible to limit the scale of an individual program to a single tree and still fulfill the basic concepts of PHC. Why the need for PHC single tree programs? In some instances, a client is concerned about the health and appearance of only one or two large specimen trees and is not interested in managing the entire landscape. Plant Health Care for a single tree typically starts with a call requesting an arborist to look at a "sick" tree. During this appointment or after a more detailed evaluation, an arborist may be able to outline a strategy to restore the tree's health and appearance. At a minimum, the PHC program should consist of a care strategy plus at least one follow-up visit to evaluate the effectiveness of the treatments. A brief report is then sent to the client after the evaluation.

Individual tactics can be presented as an itemized list identifying the price for each treatment or it can be presented as a package with a single price. The advantage of an itemized listing is that the client can prioritize where their money will be spent. They may elect to have the tree sprayed, for example, but decide not to have recommended fertilizing and pruning implemented. The disadvantage of itemizing is that the client might elect to have only some of the treatments performed thus reducing effectiveness of the overall strategy. It is far more effective to group all treatments that are essential to the tree's care in a single package.

EXAMPLE OF TREE MANAGEMENT PRICING

Pricing PHC tree management programs is relatively simple. The contract price incorporates a company's established rates to perform individual treatments plus a fee to conduct follow-up evaluation and prepare a short report. For example, assume a tree care company has the following rates for their services:

SERVICE	RATE
liquid injection fertilization	$7/100 square feet
pesticide spray for trees 25 to 40 feet tall	$40/tree
pruning	$75/two person crew
consulting arborist	$50/hour

These example rates assume that the tree company has already incorporated the necessary mark-ups for each service to meet targeted gross margins. With these rates in mind, consider the following simplified scenario to illustrate this pricing approach.

> *A client has a tree exhibiting a decline that can be attributed to low soil fertility and a secondary pest. The strategy is to manage the pest with a pesticide application while restoring vitality by increasing soil fertility. In addition, the tree needs to be pruned to remove the dead and dying branches. After these treatments are completed, an evaluation visit will be made at the end of the season to assess the effectiveness of the strategy and determine what may be needed in the following year.*

Based upon the tree's size and condition, the rates for the pesticide application, fertilizing, pruning and evaluation are $40, $110, $112 and $30, respectively. The contract price is $292 to implement the care strategy for the tree this year. Some companies may offer a small discount from this price as the mark-ups for each service includes cost of sale. Since the services are sold as a package, selling expenses are reduced.

LANDSCAPE MANAGEMENT APPROACH

Plant Health Care at the landscape level allows an arborist to manage plants at a larger scale. This improves care as more of the site factors and cultural practices that influence plant health come under the control of a single company. But even here, there can be several different types of landscape management. The highest level of PHC landscape management involves creating an inventory of all the woody plants on a property and establishing a maintenance contract that provides care for these same plants and inspection reports to the client after each landscape visit. Landscape management programs generally involve two individuals, a monitor who inspects the property and implements the treatments and a consulting arborist who sells the program to the client and then maintains periodic contact to ensure the program meets the client's expectations.

INVENTORIES

Inventories are an essential part of the highest level of PHC landscape management. Not only are they an excellent means of communication with the client,

> *All that is required of a landscape map is the ability of everyone responsible for a property to be able to locate a particular tree on the map.*

they are also useful for keeping treatment records on the individual plants in the landscape. The best means of maintaining inventories is with a landscape map. Typically each tree is individually identified on the map, but shrub groupings, if composed of a single species, are only identified as a group rather than individual plants. Many companies often avoid producing landscape maps because they are concerned that creating the maps will be time-consuming and be too expensive for most clients. Landscape maps do not need to be elaborate. Scale maps are not essential. All that is necessary is that everyone responsible for the property, the monitor, consulting arborist and client, can locate a particular tree from the map. As long as the map is proportional, it should fulfill the function of a landscape map. While these maps can be rendered by hand, the majority of companies using inventories have the maps generated and stored utilizing computer software. Plant Health Care companies that are allied with a landscape design/build division may find it convenient to use LAND-CADD® to create and store the maps. Less expensive options include utilizing home landscape design software packages to create maps. Storing the landscape map on a computer also allows for easy updating as the landscape changes over the years.

A consulting arborist may find it takes one or two hours to identify all woody plants in a typical 1/3 acre residential landscape and locate them on a rough map. It will take approximately another hour to create a landscape map utilizing a computer software package. Commercial maps can obviously take several times longer. The inventorying and landscape map are often billed as a separate, one time charge. Typically the charge for the map is the standard hourly rate for the consulting arborist's field time plus the cost of a clerical person's time to create the map. A copy of the landscape map, and accompanying key, is presented to the client at the beginning of the first season. If the client maintains the contract in subsequent years, and the landscape is altered, a new map can be generated. Plant Health Care managers should not underestimate the perceived value of this map to the client. It is usually the first tangible product received from the contract.

MAINTENANCE CONTRACT

The maintenance contract is for the annual care of all the woody plants in a landscape. The price is best given as a lump sum contract rather than as separate prices for individual services. Some companies have attempted to offer their landscape PHC program as separate services — an hourly charge for monitoring with separate charges for each treatment applied. The price for each service is clearly identified at the beginning of the contract, $40 per pesticide application, for example. While this approach simplifies pricing, it generally meets with much resistance from potential clients. Most clients resist paying for monitoring. They do not want to pay to have someone walk through their landscape looking for pests. In addition, they are leery of open-ended contracts that may run up an unknown and unacceptable number of charges. It is far more acceptable to offer a single contract price that encompasses at least the three services expected to be performed during the year — monitoring, pest management and client communication. Thus the client knows that the company will conduct periodic inspections of the property and perform any pesticide application needed to maintain or improve the health and appearance of the woody plants, all for an agreed upon price, regardless of what may occur.

This type of pricing requires the company to have prior knowledge of what will be needed to maintain the landscape over the coming year. If the company overestimates their expenses for the year, the client pays more than they

> *Clients are leery of open-ended contracts that may run up an unknown and unacceptable number of charges.*

need to and may decide to forgo the contract the following year. If the company underestimates its expenses, it charges less than it needed and loses money. It is critical to the success of the program that the costs of the three primary ingredients of a PHC landscape maintenance — monitoring, pest management treatments and client communication — be accurately predicted.

MONITORING

Monitoring is an essential part of PHC. Most PHC landscape maintenance programs schedule monthly monitoring visits to a property during the growing season. Monitoring is an intensive practice, but it must be done in an efficient manner. The average monitor spends about twenty to thirty-five minutes per 1/3 acre residential property and will spend about two and one-half hours to four hours at a client's property during a year. Thus if the monitoring rate is $50 per hour, the total price of monitoring a property in a region with a seven month growing season is about $180. Clients are not willing to pay large sums of money for monitoring, so this labor expense must be kept to a minimum. During a scheduled visit, the monitor must inspect the plants and record his/her observations as well as provide any necessary target applications of pesticides. While a half-hour visit may appear too brief to complete these duties, necessary tasks can be accomplished if the monitor focuses on the key plants that are most likely to require close inspection and possible treatment during a particular visit. Equally important, the means of recording observations must also be quick. Some companies employ a series of codes by which the monitor can highlight a particular plant on the landscape map. For example, if a yew has a heavy infestation of Fletcher scale and the monitor applies a pesticide to the crawlers, he or she may circle the plant on the landscape map and write FS, PO as codes to mean Fletcher scale and an application of orthene was applied. The number of codes needed to describe most problems and their treatments is not overwhelming. Most regions have perhaps twenty-five key pests and the common treatment list may be only twice or three times that long.

PESTICIDE TREATMENTS

The number of pesticide treatments needed for a particular property can be predicted by knowing the number of key plants in the landscape. Most companies develop a list of key plants in their market and key pests that afflict them, along with treatment tactics. From this list, a consulting arborist should be able to quickly predict the approximate number of pesticide applications that may be needed during the coming year. For example, if a landscape contains several birch trees, in many areas of the country it can be readily assumed that birch leaf miner treatments will need to be applied. The monitor will be applying most of the target applications during his/her scheduled visits. Pesticide treatments applied on large trees or clusters of trees or pesticide applications made at a more frequent interval than monthly, such as apple scab treatments, are usually routed and performed by an applicator other than the monitor. Since the monitor visits a landscape on a monthly basis, there are some pests, such as aphids, that may experience tremendous population growth between visits. Clients must be informed in advance, that these pests may cause minor aesthetic damage as monitors can not provide the weekly inspections that may be necessary to provide control of such pests. In addition, treatments for certain pests, such as Japanese beetles, gypsy moth and forest tent caterpillar, are sometimes excluded from a PHC landscape maintenance contract. These pests can cause extensive plant damage in a short period of time and the frequency of monitoring needed to manage these pests may not be practical.

> *Most PHC landscape maintenance programs schedule monthly monitoring visits to a property during the growing season.*

> *The number of pesticide treatments needed for a particular property can be predicted by knowing the number of key plants in the landscape.*

MONITORING REPORTS

Monitoring reports are the third essential ingredient of a maintenance contract. These reports are the primary means by which the client is made aware of what is occurring in their landscape and the management activities of the monitor. Generating inspection reports must be a simple and inexpensive task. It is difficult to write a monthly narrative report for each property a monitor visits. A more efficient method is to have a report produced from codes used in the field to record plant problems and cultural treatments that were impelmented. For example, a circled yew on the landscape map with the codes FS, PO may be written out in the inspection reports as:

Plant #	Plant	Symptoms	Problem	Treatment
JY2	Japanese yew	yellow foliage	Fletcher scale	applied orthene to reduce population

> *Monitoring reports are not limited to insect, mite and disease problems and their treatment, but should also identify environmental and cultural problems observed during monitoring.*

Monitoring reports are not limited to insect, mite and disease problems and their treatment, but should also identify environmental and cultural problems observed during monitoring. If one or more of the recommended treatments are beyond what the contract specified, vertical mulching for example, then this treatment should be identified and the consulting arborist should meet with the client to describe the additional service and discuss the benefits and price. The creation of these reports is a clerical task and should be priced at the time required to enter the appropriate remarks for each code and the cost of mailing the report.

FERTILIZING

Fertilizing is sometimes included in a maintenance contract. It is usually applied by an applicator on a route rather than the monitor during a routine visit. What will be fertilized during the year is clearly identified in the contract and only those plants so identified are treated. Some contracts are set up so that all the mature trees are fertilized on a rotating schedule so every tree is treated once every two or three years.

PRUNING

Pruning is occasionally included in a contract, but it is usually better to omit pruning and offer it as a separate work item. Pruning needs can greatly differ from year to year. The work is also more time consuming than what can be accomplished by a monitor during his/her monthly property visit. In addition, most pruning can be performed during the winter, a time when pruning crews are usually working with very little backlog. Typically, the consulting arborist meets with the client in the fall to review the year's activity and also identify any pruning needs. This work is usually itemized on the proposal and accepted items are completed during the winter.

SHEARING

Shearing can also require more work than can be accomplished during the monthly visit, thus it is best left as a separate item. Some companies include shearing in a contract since improper shearing can increase many pest problems as well as adversely affect a plant's health. This activity is performed by a separate crew at the established hourly rate for a crew. Time required for the shearing is estimated and that total is added into the price of the maintenance contract.

EXAMPLE OF LANDSCAPE MANAGEMENT PRICING

The pricing of a PHC landscape maintenance contract will be similar to that demonstrated in the following example utilizing the rates identified in the single tree management program. Assuming the growing season is from April to October, the property will require seven monitoring visits with each visit taking approximately forty minutes including drive time. The hourly rate for the monitor is $50 for a total of $233. The landscape consists of a large variety of key plants so the anticipated number of treatments are twelve, ten of which can be performed by the monitor during a scheduled visit. Two of the treatments are for a foliage disease so these are best routed with other properties requiring the same treatments. The two fungicide applications follow the established rate of $40 per application. The other ten are target applications made with a backpack spray, thus the price for these is $10 each (the labor cost is already included in the monitoring time). The clerical staff will require a little under two hours during the season to generate and send the reports at a rate of $15 per hour. Finally the consulting arborist will be meeting with the client for about an hour to review the program at the end of the season. The price of the program would be:

monitoring	$232.00
target applications	100.00
routed applications	80.00
reports	28.00
consulting arborist	50.00
Program Price	$440.00

> *By incorporating lawn care activities such as turf fertilizing and pesticide treatments into a PHC package, all management decisions regarding the soil are within one company.*

The landscape maintenance program can be modified in one or more ways. Some companies are taking the concept of landscape management a little further by incorporating lawn care activities such as turf fertilizing and pesticide treatments into their package. From a plant care standpoint, this is advantageous as it places all management decisions regarding the soil within one company. This helps avoid the problem of a lawn care company applying a fertilizer one day and the tree care company applying it again the next. The advantage to the client is having to discuss the care of their landscape with only one individual. While some tree care companies have created their own divisions to provide lawn care, most subcontract the work, but still review and approve cultural treatments.

Another approach is to simplify the landscape management contract as a means to decrease the cost and increase sales volume. While offering the "full scale" program, some companies also offer a separate program that involves monitoring at a less frequent interval (meaning the optimum time to treat a pest may be missed). While pesticide treatments are still included in the contract, monitoring reports are eliminated or much reduced. Communication is often through door hangers that identify what was treated during a particular visit. No landscape maps or treatment record are kept (beyond what is required by EPA). This decreases the time it takes to inspect the property since observations do not need to be recorded and office expenses can be eliminated if reports are not sent. Using the property illustrated in the example above, the price of this program would be:

monitoring	$150.00
target application	70.00
routed applications	80.00
program price	$300.00

One of the most important considerations when developing PHC programs is that several levels of programs be offered. Equally important, each program must maintain the same level of profitability for the company.

CHAPTER SUMMARY

- Plant Health Care should offer an array of programs to fit the client needs and expectations rather than the other way around.
- Plant Health Care reaches its fullest potential when an entire landscape is managed, but it is possible to limit individual programs to a single tree and still fulfill basic PHC concepts.
- Plant Health Care at the landscape level allows an arborist to manage plants at a larger scale, which improves care as more of the site factors and cultural practices that influence plant health are controlled by a single company.
- Site inventories and the creation of a landscape map are essential parts of PHC management.
- The price for an annual PHC maintenance contract is best given as a lump sum rather than as separate prices for individual services.
- Annual PHC contracts should include at least monitoring, pest management and client communication. It is critical that the costs of these three ingredients be accurately predicted.

CHAPTER 7

PHC Monitoring and Inventory

INTRODUCTION

> *Too frequently landscape professionals are called to provide "first aid" therapy for plants with obvious, advanced problems...*

As described earlier, Plant Health Care parallels modern human health maintenance because it combines and integrates tactics for both treating existing problems (therapy) and preventing future problems. PHC emphasizes prevention as a primary principle. Too frequently, landscape professionals are called to provide "first aid" therapy for plants with obvious, advanced problems, when prompt, earlier involvement using PHC strategies could have circumvented or minimized the problem condition. Because multiple strategies are combined, adoption of a successful PHC campaign is a challenge that hinges on thorough, comprehensive planning for each step of the approach. An arborist ready to accept that challenge needs complete directions for putting a PHC program into practice.

While each PHC program will be custom-designed to meet the specific needs of an individual client, the practical application of the approach always relies on selection and integration from among a broad range of strategies aimed at protecting and enhancing tree health. There are some common principles and program components that underlie PHC implementation in every instance. The remainder of this book outlines the scope and organization of a complete PHC program, and specifically details each step an arborist will consider when implementing and managing a PHC-based service.

MONITORING

PHC demands intelligent decision making on the part of the arborist, so that the best management strategy for a given site can be efficiently selected from all available choices. **Monitoring** is an essential activity in a PHC program that guides and directs this constant decision-making process. Information must be gathered about the condition of a client's plants, and the client's desires and expectations regarding plant maintenance. The monitor uses this information to recommend specific treatment or maintenance activities in the landscape.

Monitoring, not treating, is the scheduled activity in PHC. Treatments are prescribed and then scheduled only when monitoring determines they are needed.

Observations and inspections during the spring, summer and fall will provide data to more accurately forecast plant problems, make diagnoses, assess potential damage, select from alternative treatment methods and evaluate the PHC system. Figure 7-1 shows an example of a checklist on which the monitor records information during inspections. This information can later be transferred to a monitoring report which may be sent to the client (Figure 7-2).

SCHEDULED MONITORING

> *Scheduled visits are needed to observe and record developmental changes.*

Weather conditions, especially temperature and rainfall, may vary on individual properties within the same locale, and will certainly vary from region to region. Every site varies in the environmental resources (both excess and deficits) available. Macro-climate and micro-climate changes can initiate plant stress. Climatic factors alter greatly the annual development of plants and plant problems. These environmental conditions also change the competitive advantages of neighboring plants and animals throughout the year. Scheduled visits are needed to observe and record these developmental changes.

Scheduled visits may enable the monitor to avoid treatment. Not all problems occur at the same intensity or severity on related plants. Cultivars, varieties and species within the same genus vary in susceptibility to stress problems. Monitors will prescribe treatments for only those plants likely to show visual reactions reaching a threshold under prevailing climatic conditions.

Scheduled visits may enable the monitor to properly time treatments. Not all problems arise at the same time during the year. Not all treatments are effective throughout the year. Climatic conditions are unpredictable. By noting macro-climatic changes, anticipating micro-climate changes on the specific site, and understanding tree reactions to environmental changes, the monitor can prescribe specifically timed treatments for specific plants that maximize effectiveness. Prescriptions can be made to ensure treatments and plant reactions together generate positive and effective changes.

For example, some pests have developmental stages extremely susceptible to treatments while other life-stages are resistant to treatments. By understanding the plant/environment interactions, low impact treatments using environmentally-sensitive techniques can minimize plant stress. Ignoring plant reactions and their environmental context could lead to massive impact, expensive and poorly timed treatments which could have no effect on the targeted stress problem and might initiate many additional problems. Ineffective treatments are wastes of time, money, and materials while polluting or convoluting a Plant Health Care program.

Monitors need to examine key plants and key stress problems on a periodic basis. The time between monitoring visits must be timed to a biological/developmental calendar, not necessarily measured in evenly spaced weeks or months. Plant reactions to changing environmental conditions determine periodicity of monitoring visits. For example, some insect stress problems arise from multiple generations of the pest per growing season. Each generation's effect on the plant (that reaches a management threshold) must be effectively minimized. Using insect traps can assist monitors to assess plant health over time.

Scheduled monitoring allows the monitor to alter treatments. The **threshold** varies with time of year. Less severe stress problems that occur late in the growing season may be controlled with environmentally-milder treatments. Spot treatments can be used and still be effective.

Since PHC is based on the assessment of potential severity, the monitor must keep records of any stress problem present, the increase or decrease throughout the year, influence of beneficial biological and environmental conditions, pesticides used, and effects of applied treatments on each property throughout the year. This along with prior years records and environmental data will allow better and safer treatments to be used in the future.

PUBLIC OR CLIENT RELATIONS

While the salesperson or owner/manager may have been the individual most closely associated or involved with clients in the past, the monitor becomes the firm's key contact throughout the growing season in the PHC program. With small firms, the owner/operator may also be the monitor. With larger firms the monitor and the salesperson should communicate frequently and precisely. Each must know what has been recommended to the client in order to avoid confusion and misunderstandings. The client must trust both the salesperson and the monitor, and must feel confident in the monitor's expertise and communication with the salesperson. Through frequency of visits, the monitor is in a position to earn more trust than is the salesperson, and should always see this as an opportunity to build goodwill for the company.

Sales is not an essential function of the monitor. In some firms they sell, in others they do not. Requirements for arboricultural services are often readily evident as the monitor performs the inspections, however, and suggestions for treatment can be offered to the client during the scheduled visit or in follow-up correspondence.

ROUTINE MONITORING

Routine monitoring has been divided into four categories: detection surveys, risk management surveys, biological evaluations, and treatment evaluations.

> *Routine monitoring has been divided into four categories: detection surveys, risk management surveys, biological evaluations, and treatment evaluations.*

- **Detection surveys** involve determining stress problems damaging the tree including insects, diseases, mechanical damage, drought, and chemicals.
- **Risk management surveys** include information on insect populations and distribution, disease severity and intensity, and the damage caused by other stress factors.
- **Biological evaluations** involve assessment of environmental influences on stress development now and into the future.
- **Treatment evaluations** are completed to assess treatment effectiveness and suggest alternative treatments or treatment modifications needed.

These activities by monitors are more fully described in the following pages.

Inspections by monitors are primarily visual. In PHC, it is the plant's reaction to stress conditions that are observed. For example, there are many insects present on the bark of a tree. Some will be beneficial, some are just passing bye and have no effect on the tree, and others may be of a pest species. In this case, if the tree is not reacting to environmental changes initiated by the pest species at some management threshold, no problem exists and treatments should not be prescribed. Insects and their highly characteristic damage can be used for identification and monitoring, but it is plant stress reaching a threshold that must be observed, recorded, and an effective treatment prescribed.

MONITORING CHECKLIST
[attach copy of inventory map/checklist]

[PHC COMPANY IDENTIFICATION]:
PHC Client Name:
Date of Site Visit:
Monitor on Duty:

Key plants on site (list-use 2-letter plant ID codes to designate):
Number of plants present:
Location on site:
Key stress:
- General or specific stress problems:
- Pests/cultural problems evident?
- Specific Identification—insects, mites, diseases, cultural conditions:
- Need for treatment or maintenance projected?

Treatment steps taken during site visit:
Additional recommendations to be made:

Other plant species on site (list):
Number of plants present:
Location on site:
Condition:
- General or specific stress problems:
- Pests/cultural problems evident?
- Specific Identification—insects, mites, diseases, cultural conditions:
- Need for treatment or maintenance projected?

Treatment steps taken during site visit:

Samples Taken During Site Visit:
Soil Analysis:
- location on site:
- pH reading:
- mineral analysis:

Additional recommendations to be made:
For Treatment of Existing Problems:
For Preventitive Maintenance:
Additional Maintenance/Cultural Recommendations Proposed:

Other Information:

Figure 7 - 1. Suggested content for a *Monitoring Checklist.*

MONITORING REPORT

[copy of personalized inventory map attached for reference to species and location information]

[PHC COMPANY LETTERHEAD]

PHC Client:
Address of Site:

PHC Monitor :
Date of Site Visit:
Time of Site Visit:

Trees and Shrubs Monitored:

Status/Condition:

Maintenance or Treatment Steps Taken:

Further Recommendations:

Next Monitoring Inspection Scheduled for:

Figure 7 - 2. Suggested content for a *Monitoring Report* to be sent to the client.

Monitors must be aware and be continually updated on changing environmental roles pest species may play in tree health, especially when exotic pests are introduced. Experience and observational skills are the critical tools of the monitor. For example, many insects, both pests and beneficials, are large enough to be readily seen with the unaided eye. Other insects leave eggs, frass, or plant symptoms sufficiently distinctive to identify the cause of damage. Some insects and mites can be observed with a hand lens. **Diseases** are mostly microscopic, requiring laboratory observations for positive identification, but often cause characteristic symptoms on host plants.

Other approaches used by monitors to detect problems include traps, phenological data, degree day information and predictive modeling. Sticky traps have been used to lower insect populations, but primarily serve as an efficient indicator of insect presence and abundance. Environmental data are sufficient for a few insects and diseases to be able to predict severity of damage.

MATERIALS NEEDED FOR MONITORING

There are certain items that are needed to make the task of monitoring as productive as possible in as limited a time span as adequate. These items include:

- **A supply of plastic bags.** The plastic bags should be large enough to store at least one 6 inch long branch with foliage and be able to be tied so that the insects inside cannot escape.
- **Containers.** Small containers similar to those used for prescription drugs are convenient for collecting soft-bodied insects.
- **Label tags.** A label tag should be inserted within each plastic bag containing a sample or placed on containers. The tag should be large enough so that a waterproof pen can be used to write the land-owner's name, date sample was taken, city, and collector's name.
- **Waterproof writing pen.**
- **Coring (not auger) soil probe.**
- **Hand Trowel.**
- **Hand lens.** A hand lens is needed to examine small insects. Because it is so easy to drop or misplace the small lens, it is always a good idea to attach a heavy duty string to the lens so that it can be placed around the neck.
- **Small knife.** Sometimes it is necessary to pry off an insect covering so that a closer examination can be possible. A small knife is a useful tool for this purpose as well as for use to dissect an insect case.
- **Pruning shears.** Pruning shears must always be used to remove a small plant sample. Breaking off a branch leaves a jagged end and often the bark is torn. It is important that the shears be kept sharp.
- **Recording book.** Record keeping is one of the most important elements of a good scouting program. Without good records, the whole program may be a failure. A record book should be large enough to adequately store all the pertinent information about each site that is monitored.

It is nearly impossible for even a professional entomologist, plant pathologist, horticulturist, or forester to recognize all the different kinds of insects, diseases, or stress situations that impact trees and shrubs. So it is not uncommon to discover stress that one does not recognize. In order to get a correct identification, it is important to take a plant, pest, or soil sample.

BACKGROUND EDUCATION OR TRAINING

> *Monitoring requires training and education in many fields of biology...*

Monitoring for PHC is labor intensive and expensive. Monitoring requires training and education in many fields of biology and acute observation skills. The monitor must be able to identify plants, know how a healthy plant looks and functions, recognize sick or abnormal plants, know the likely causes of abnormalities, know tactics that will return the plant to a healthy condition, and be able to choose the treatment most likely to be effective without raising environmental risks or hazards. Individuals best trained to be monitors are college-educated and have an Associate or Bachelor of Science or equivalent degree in a discipline, such as horticulture, which promotes plant familiarity. Personal training by a qualified arboriculture PHC monitor can provide the skills sufficient for individuals to serve in local areas where the key plant and key stress list is limited.

INVENTORY THE SITE

> *Timely site visits are essential to an effective PHC program and an accurate site inventory will prevent these site visits from becoming prohibitively expensive.*

Timely site visits for monitoring, as described in the previous section, are essential to an effective PHC program with emphasis on preventative tree health care. Maintenance of a thorough, up-to-date, accurate site inventory will prevent these site visits from becoming prohibitively expensive, because a strong inventory will streamline and direct the monitor's efforts. A good inventory will pinpoint tasks that require action, and help troubleshoot future work to be completed on site.

One strong advantage of PHC is that it can provide a health maintenance plan for the total landscape, including turf, foundation plantings, shrubs, and other plants, as well as the large trees an arborist is more commonly concerned with. The PHC site inventory, therefore, includes all plants on a site. The site inventory is a tool that will help to maximize time efficiency for the monitor and improve control over potential problems on the site. This comprehensive inventory will include identification of landscape plants, identification of key plants, key stresses, a record of site specific features, and a map to record all of this information for repeated future reference. Each of these components are vital to the success of routine monitoring efforts.

IDENTIFY THE LANDSCAPE PLANTS

IMPORTANCE OF ACCURATE PLANT IDENTIFICATION

A monitor must be able to recognize and key-out plant characteristics at any time of the year, since accurate identification of all trees and shrubs monitored is critical to predict future problems or diagnose current symptoms. Trees of a given species will be susceptible to a predictable set of cultural and biological problems, and species that are closely related (in the same botanical family) may exhibit similar responses to stress, and may respond in the same way to a treatment strategy. Species identifications will become part of the site inventory, and will be accessed continually to plan treatment schedules and subsequent customer reports. Plant identification is required prior to application of some targeted pesticides, and identification is also a vital component of a tree value assessment.

Landscape plants need to be identified in terms of the ***scientific name*** (***genus***, ***species***, and [when required] ***cultivar***), as well as by common name (clients may use only a known common name). While the scientific name is constant, common names are too confusing to aid in inventory management, since one plant may be labeled by several different common names in different geographic locations. For example, the name *Platanus occidentalis* identifies the genus (*Platanus*) and species (*occidentalis*) of a popular landscape tree that may go by common names of American Planetree, Planetree, Sycamore, or Buttonwood depending on the region of the country in which it is located.

Tree identification is based on classification and recognition of key features of the plant's ***anatomy*** and ***morphology***. Accurate identification of woody landscape trees and shrubs will require training, since the monitor must have the background to recognize identification features of plants, and some knowledge of how to use simple classification keys. A skilled arborist will be able to pool information from a range of characteristics to arrive at an identification. Excellent botanical and horticultural reference manuals which describe the identification characteristics, and other ornamental and cultural features, are available to supplement (but not completely replace) training in identification skills.

Full courses, workshop series, or mini-courses that offer training in landscape plants identification are available through most major universities and colleges with programs in agriculture, horticulture, or urban forestry. Excellent programs are also available at many junior colleges, or through adult-education classes held in local high schools or community centers. Many progressive arboriculture firms also offer in-house training programs for their employees.

Identification keys (based on woody plant ***taxonomy***) are arranged such that each criterion or evaluation point can be considered in a sequence, to determine the correct plant identification by process of elimination. This is much like a game of 20 questions, except there will be far more than 20 questions, and one false answer will tend to lead the user far astray from his objective of correct plant identification. Keys are most useful if the user is well versed in the botanical terms used to construct the key, and unfortunately, a simple key usually cannot account for all "exceptions to the rule" that exist in a natural range of a woody species. So while a general understanding of classification keys and the terms used in them will help an arborist or other landscape manager with identification, a botanical key is seldom the best way to accurately pinpoint the identity of an unknown woody plant in the landscape.

Alternatively, good woody plant identification manuals organize a range of morphological features to allow consideration of plant features one by one, narrow down possible choices, and gradually determine a species identification. The most useful tools for identification are reference manuals that describe botanical and taxonomic identification terms, include drawings of alternative identification features, and are geared toward the specific geographic region of interest. Several excellent reference manuals specifically useful for landscape plant identification and inventory construction are noted in Chapter 9 - Technical Resources. Again, a reference is only a supplemental aid to thorough training and field experience in woody plant identification.

Within a PHC operation, a standardized, abbreviated (two letter) code list for tree and shrub species common to the area should be provided to each staff monitor, to guarantee uniformity in recording and allow easier labeling of maps and other documents related to the site.

FEATURES USED IN WOODY PLANT IDENTIFICATION

Leaf type and leaf arrangement are obvious and useful identification features (although only valid for part of the year for deciduous trees). Other useful plant

> *Good woody plant identification manuals organize a range of morphological features to allow plantsmen to determine a species identification.*

attributes include size, habit, bud type, fruit morphology and type, color, texture, and others.

Leaf and bud arrangement is typically the first feature used in keying out the identity of an unknown tree or shrub species. There are four categories for use in categorizing plant groups:

- *opposite*—leaves emerge in pairs, directly across from each other
- *alternate*—leaves emerge singly along the length of a stem and are not paired
- *subopposite*—leaves are not directly opposite each other, but pairs of leaves may be closely spaced
- *whorled*—three buds occur at a single node.

The leaf arrangement feature is clearly identifiable whether or not the plant is in leaf at the time of identification, because the buds maintain the arrangement pattern (Figure 7-3). This initial identification feature provides an easy, quick way to narrow the possible identities of an individual tree, by eliminating many species from consideration right away.

During seasons when the tree is in leaf, the leaf type provides another strong identification clue (Figure 7-3). Simple leaves describe cases when a bud is located in the axil subtended by a single leaf. Compound leaves occur when the bud is located in the axil of a structure with multiple leaflets. Leaves may be compound pinnate (leaflets are spaced out along both sides of the structure [rachis] like the teeth of a comb) or compound palmate (leaflets all originate at a single point, like the spokes of an umbrella). Leaves may also be bipinnately compound, which is simply a more intricate variation of a pinnately compound leaf.

Other leaf characteristics that can be useful identification features include the leaf margin (smooth and entire, lobed, or serrated), the shape of the leaf base where it connects with the petiole, or the presence of pubescence (hairs or fuzz) on the lower or upper leaf surfaces.

Coniferous (cone-bearing) trees (e.g., pines or junipers) may be distinguished from angiosperms (most broad-leaved, usually deciduous trees) by their unusual leaf types (Figure 7-3). Conifer leaves may be needle-like (long and pointed), awl-like (usually sharp at the tip, and shaped like an awl), or scale-like (overlapping leaves like scales on a fish, and usually not sharp at the tip).

During the growing season, the young current season's growth (twigs) may have a **characteristic color** or **pubescence** that give additional clues for identification. Seasonal features (e.g., brilliant fall foliage color or highly-pigmented foliage during the leafing-out period in the spring) are characteristics for some species. During the dormant seasons, the buds themselves can be distinguished based on an amazing number of fine points such as the presence of bud-scale ridges, bud shape and color, leaf scar appearance, or scent. To distinguish closely related species, sometimes even the characteristics of the pith (chambered or solid) might be considered as an identification feature.

Flowers and fruits are identification features during their brief seasons of display. Their colors, size, fruit type and morphology (e.g., dry or flesh-coated; drupes, berries or pomes), showiness, fragrance, persistence, and seasons of availability can all become part of an identification for an individual plant species. Again, good woody plant identification manuals will include illustrations of each of the alternative identification features, as well as drawings specific to each plant species.

Some arborists are more skilled at initially identifying tree species "from a distance" (based on large-scale morphological features) than using the fine-scale identification characteristics that have been described above to resolve

> *Useful identification features include: leaf type, leaf arrangement, size, habit, bud type, fruit morphology and type, color, texture.*

68 / THE PLANT HEALTH CARE MANAGEMENT SYSTEM

Anatomy of a simple leaf.

Leaf arrangements on a stem.

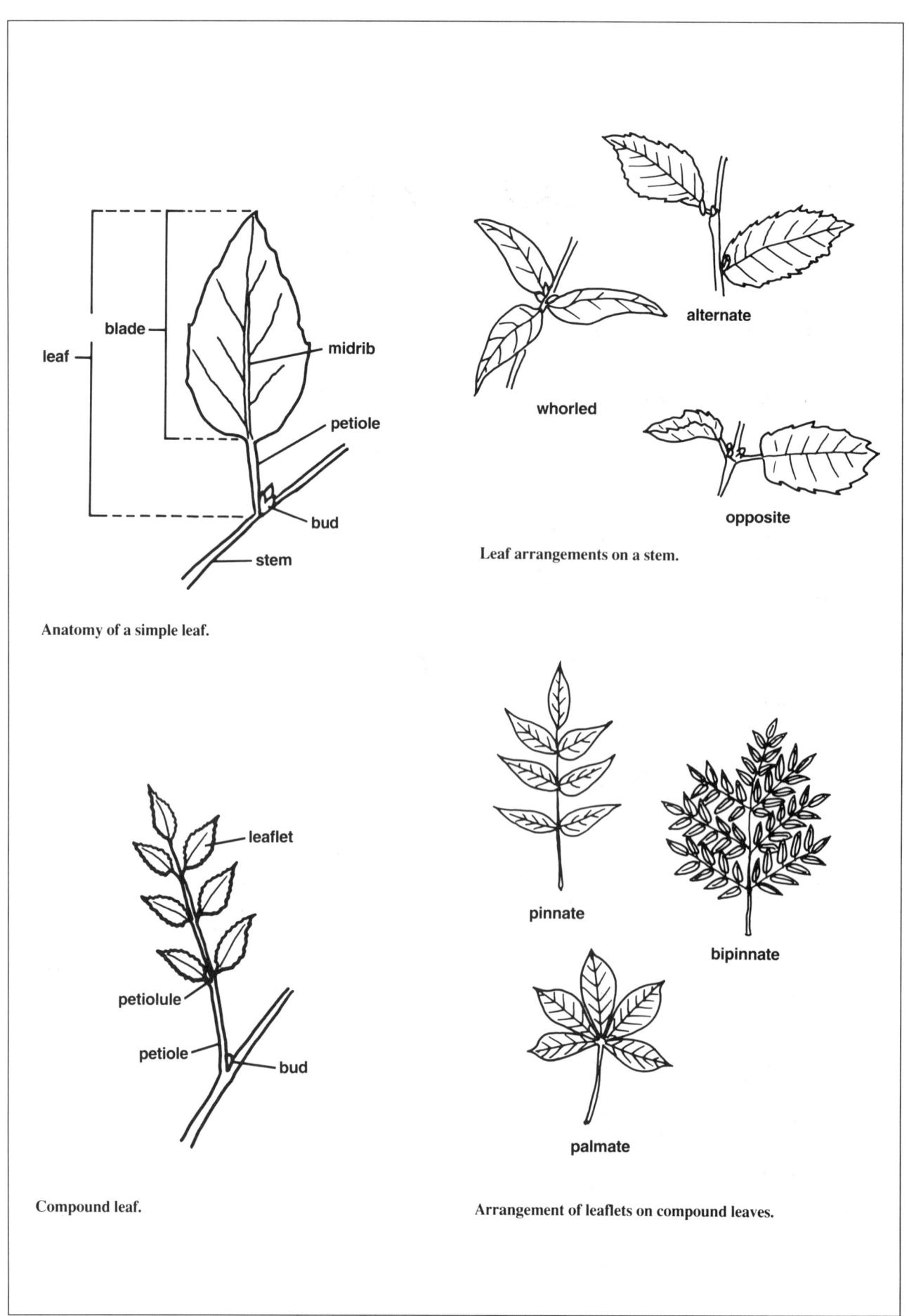

Compound leaf.

Arrangement of leaflets on compound leaves.

Figure 7 - 3. Characteristics used for plant identification purposes.

PHC MONITORING AND INVENTORY / 69

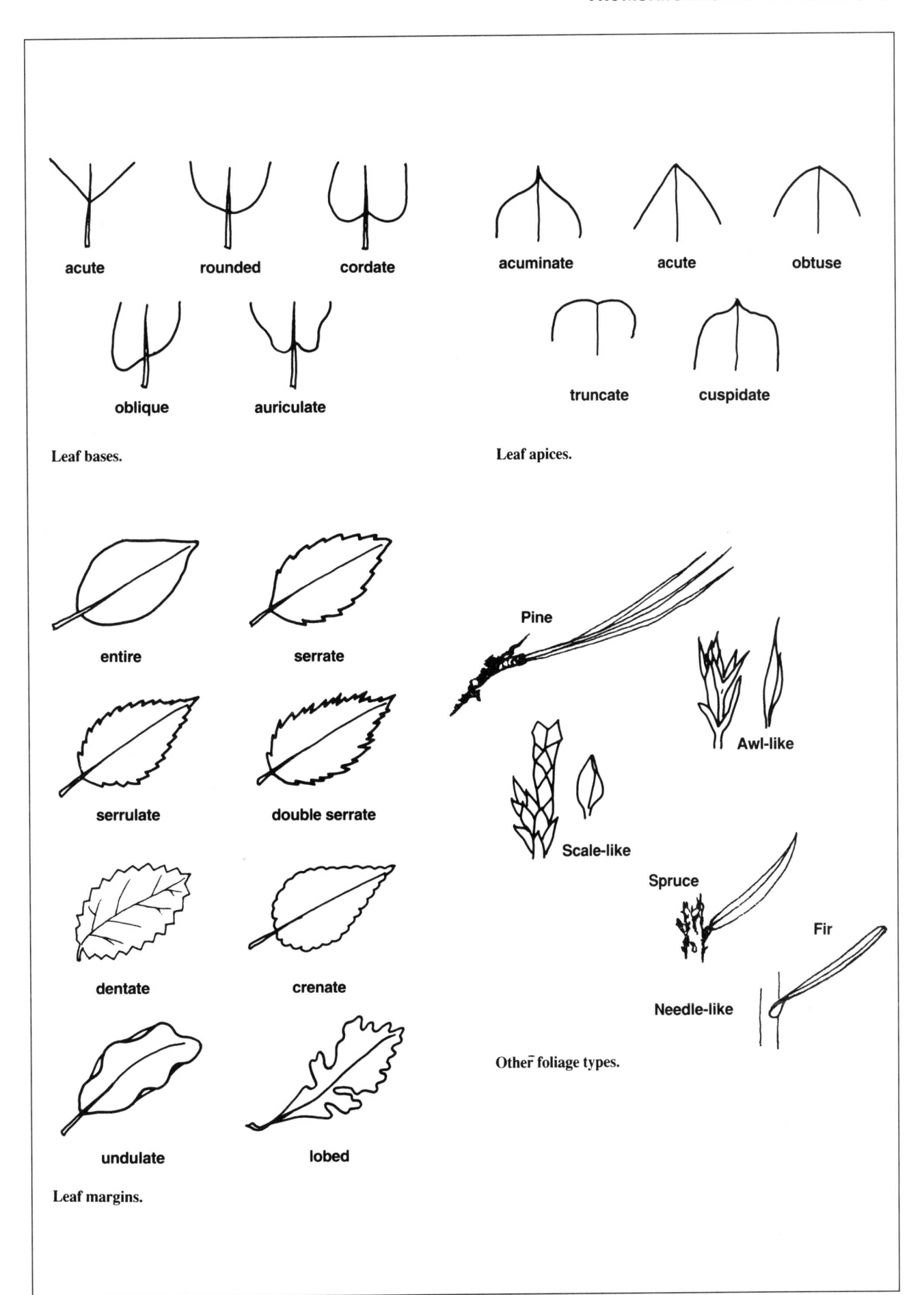

Leaf bases.

Leaf apices.

Leaf margins.

Other foliage types.

Figure 7 - 3 *continued.*

individual species and cultivar differences. Growth habit, for example, describes the overall shape of the silhouette outline of a tree or shrub. Some species are easy to identify based on their strong, characteristic habit, such as the cone-shaped outline of a blue spruce, the weeping habit of a willow, or the broad-rounded canopy of a red maple. Branching habit, that is, whether the branches extend out horizontally from the main trunk of a tree, or ascend at a certain angle upward, will help identify certain trees. Overall plant size is also an obvious key, as well as foliage texture or color traits. Some species are easily recognizable based on ornamental bark color and texture (e.g. white birch, corktree, sycamore, musclewood).

A broad range of identification features can be used to help accurately identify a landscape plant. The skill of the arborist comes into play as multiple criteria are considered during an identification, and the speed and accuracy of this skill improves with repeated practice.

Once all plants are identified, a form, similar to the one shown in Figure 7-4 can be used to record the information.

IDENTIFY KEY PLANTS, KEY STRESSES

The concept of "*key plants*" recognizes that certain genera or species are significantly more prone to attack by predictable stress than other plants, more frequently exhibit sensitivity to cultural problems, or are more sensitive or significant in the client's mind. When the PHC site inventory identifies one of these key plants, it immediately alerts the practicing arborist to concentrate management attention on these "hot spots," to circumvent problems before they become insurmountable.

One of the big differences between IPM in the agricultural industry, and PHC in the landscape industry, is that in agricultural crop production, acres are devoted to a single species of plant, usually with two or three primary pests associated with crop damage. IPM has, then, only a simple monitoring and scouting requirement to identify important disease or insect problems on the

---

PLANT INFORMATION

Information collection for individual plants on property (repeat this checklist for each species on site)
- genus, species, cultivar identification
- number/code (corresponding to landscape map)
- size
- location on the property
- number of same species
  — on site
  — on adjacent properties
- potential key plant/key stress?
- site information
- value assessment (with formula)
- key plant identification

Figure 7-4. Recommended content of a *Plant Information* form

crop, and keep damage below some threshold. In the landscape, however, the aesthetic and psychological value of the property is tied into the diversity of woody and other plants on a site. Scores of different plant species may exist together in a single landscape, each with the potential for damage by a different set of stress problems. The abundance of potential problem situations for an arborist to cope with—interactions between landscape plants and one of their possible stress disorders—can quickly seem overwhelming.

The only way that an arborist can manage this diversity in a practical way is to focus management efforts on the key plants found on the property, and predict the *key stress* typically associated with these plants. The diversity in a landscape might at first seem like an obstacle to PHC practices, requiring an unwieldy range of identification, diagnoses and management tasks. But in reality, only a few key plants will have a few major stress problems, which typically exist and re-occur on a site. Key plants tend to dominate management measures, and suffer persistent problems. They tend to be more likely to suffer stress and damage under a broad range of conditions, and in a variety of landscape settings. Key plants tend to cost more to maintain. Key plants can become the planned focus of management efforts, which streamlines tasks within a landscape property, concentrates time spent on certain species, and helps to control costs associated with a PHC program.

Each geographical area has its own list of problem-prone plants. For example, in the eastern United States, a thorough analysis of landscape problems by extension specialists or trained monitors over a three year period clearly identified particular genera (*Malus*, *Pyrancantha*, *Cornus*, *Prunus*, and *Rosa*) which accounted for most of the maintenance work, in a region with over 30,000 different landscape species total! The frequency of maintenance problems on these key plants was not, however, necessarily related to the concentration or frequency of planting in the landscape (Raupp et al., 1985; see Chapter 9 for complete citation). In addition, only ten key insects were responsible for 75% of the insect problems for landscape owners. These observations illustrate that identification and management of only a relatively small number of stress problems were sufficient for effective control. The same key plants presented continuing and repeated problems for residential landscape settings, public landscapes, and in a production nursery.

Again, key plants, and their associated common stress problems, must be identified for each geographic region. A "problem plant" in one geographic location may be relatively benign in another setting, where it is more tolerant of ambient conditions (soil type, pH, climate, etc.) which influence susceptibility to stress. An arborist's own accurate records over time document exactly how much time and resources were spent in the management of individual landscape problems. These records, along with up-to-date local extension reports, will help construct key plant lists for an area. See Chapter 9 (Technical Resources) for further information on the key plant concept, and for sources of key plant listings in your area.

Once the key plants are recognized and accounted for, each of the other steps in a thorough PHC program, as outlined in this manual, is streamlined. Key plants are identified during the monitoring procedure, which allows future monitoring of the landscape to zero-in on these same specimens during future site visits. Key plants are likely to incur problems year after year. Key plants demand intervention to circumvent problems. Rather than simply reacting to a problem situation, the key plants approach allows for greater planning of management strategies. The total amount of management (in particular, chemical applications) can be substantially curbed with attention to exactly the area(s) in need of intensive management.

> *Each geographical area has it own list of problem-prone plants.*

> *Key plants are identified, which allows monitoring of the landscape to zero-in on these same specimens during future site visits.*

In particular, key plants with recurrent problems are excellent targets for the PHC approach, since usually it is these plants that require excessive time and money put into repetitive standard spray efforts. One of the important start-up steps in PHC has been called "*a key stress concept*" (Olkowski and Olkowski, 1983; see Chapter 9). Stress conditions need to be prioritized, usually based on their association with key plants and the likelihood of repeat occurrences. These problem situations are specifically targeted for practice of PHC principles. A key stress could be an insect, a weed, a disease, or a vertibrate pest. A key stress could also be flooding, drought, or chemical damage.

To understand fully the key stress concept, a brief mention of plant stress development is required. Plants are influenced by many internal and external causes of stress and strain. Causes of stress can be classified as predominately physical, mechanical, biological, chemical, genetic, or ecological. All plants are in some way constrained by stress from reaching full expression of their genetic potential. Plant reactions to most stress components have been well-integrated into growth and development processes. Other stress components initiate plant reactions that can be seen as distinct symptoms. The results of all the many genetic and environmental interactions produce the plant that we see.

Moment by monent the environment changes. These changes are identified by physical, chemical and biological sensors in the plant and the plant reacts to these changes. Plant reactions change the environment. In the key stress concept, we identify major shifts in plant/environment interactions currently occurring *and* develop expectations of future shifts. Some plant reactions signify increasing levels of stress, given owner objectives. On-site evaluations help establish the dominant stress components controlling plant survival and growth, and the associated functions and values produced. The key stress components can be itemized for individual plants, groups of plants and whole landscapes.

The key stress concept is not a general listing of what stress components are present or potentially could be present, rather key stress components are listed that dominate and dictate plant reactions and represent the initiating factor in most of the plant reactions visible. The are many stress components on every site and with every plant. Few stress components represent a major quality of life change for a plant. Identify, record, monitor, and prepare treatment alternatives for those stress components actually initiating most of the negative plant reactions.

Every site has only a finite level of available resources and the various forms of plants present must make use of these resources effectively and efficiently. Plants interfere with each other and interact with the environment using inherent genetic rules. Most plants have no significant stress problems other than those shared across the site in general. A few plants may have specific problems that control their survival, growth, and appearance on a site.

The practical application of the key stress concept is that not all plant stress components, nor all plant individuals or species must be treated. Prescribe treatments once management objective thresholds are met, and then only to the intensity and extent required by the specific problem. Wide-spread, non-targeted, area treatments are usually not cost-effective nor valuable to the long-term health of landscape plants.

Identifying and prioritizing key stress components help you effectively manage site resources as well as plant values and functions. A selective, prescribed approach to stress alleviation provides an opportunity to affect plant health, save time and money, and enhance environmental quality.

> *Causes of stress can be classified as predominately physical, mechanical, biological chemical, genetic or ecological.*

DEVELOPING STRATEGIES

To target a certain key plant/key stress situation for practicing PHC tactics, information is collected first. The problem situation is identified (through site visits and the inventory). Past records of the particular site (details on how the problem was handled in previous years) and literature records establish that a particular key plant/key stress situation is a recurrent problem (conventional practices have not solved the problem). In particular, information documenting the high costs for management of the problem in the past, environmental hazards associated with the problem treatment, or client complaints (about the stress or about the treatments used) will support the case that past management strategies have been inadequate. This information collection step toward key stress identification establishes that the situation under consideration is a worthy candidate for an alternative, concerted PHC strategy for solution. Information about the stress and all the potential solutions to alleviate damage or injury to the plant is collected. Any obstacles to particular management methods (for example, cost constraints, hazards, or restrictions to the use of particular pesticides in the location) are outlined.

With all the information in hand, full-scale PHC strategies are applied to the key plant/key stress problem. The key plant is recurrently monitored to identify injury levels and the conditions on the site. Alternative management tactics are implemented in appropriate seasons. The effectiveness of the alternative management strategies and the feasibility of program implementation (relative costs versus ability of the new PHC tactics to reduce injuries or suppress pests) are evaluated. Political ramifications (response of the clients affected by the new management techniques) are assessed. Once the success of the PHC approach is thoroughly documented (by comparing the past history with the current, alternative management of a recurrent key plant/key stress problem), support for an expanded PHC program will be encouraged. These initial PHC approaches targeted for key plants/key stress help establish support and cooperation for the entire strategy. Successful PHC for one or two key plants can be the catalyst to facilitate a move toward a program of total PHC for an entire landscape. Arborists and other landscape professionals should capitalize on the obvious, clear-cut success record for PHC as regards key plants/key stress to build a foundation for adoption of PHC strategies for the entire landscape.

While tree care professionals may streamline their current efforts by making use of knowledge of key plants/key stress, they may have an opportunity to improve future landscape situations by making practical selection choices for future landscapes. When PHC practitioners are consulted for landscape plant replacements or re-landscaping jobs, they can help to "break the cycle" of recurrent stress management problems by selecting only plants that are inherently free of the typical problems. Landscapes that are constructed using plants that are relatively problem-free will have much lower maintenance requirements, and provide more consistent aesthetic benefits without the liabilities of stress on landscape specimens.

RECORD SITE SPECIFICS

PHC specialists will require detailed *site information* about each landscape under their jurisdiction, in order to maintain the plants efficiently. Site specifics will include information related to the local climate (temperature, light intensity, wind and rainfall data as well as changes imposed by urban microcli-

> *PHC specialists will require detailed site information about each landscape under their jurisdiction.*

mates), and information about the soil supporting the landscape plantings. Each of these factors influence the health and stability (adaptability) of the landscape plants and their inherent susceptibility to stress problems. Numerous physiological dysfunctions are really a reaction of a woody plant to unfavorable site conditions, and can be very difficult to diagnose unless site conditions are well researched.

Climate and soil conditions also influence the best choices for plant health maintenance. For example, they will dictate the ideal irrigation frequency, or determine the best timing or season for application of a pesticide. The plant care professional can modify the effects of local climate on landscape plants through maintenance techniques. Although tree care professionals have little control over the existing soil on site, several practices (irrigation and mulching, for example) can help alleviate unfavorable soil conditions. This is why professionals must critically consider all relevant site factors before predicting future problems in the landscape, conducting a diagnosis, or evaluating the merit of a given treatment method. A detailed checklist (Figure 7-5) can provide guidelines for collecting site information.

SITE FACTORS: CLIMATE

Temperature. Although most people know that different plant species differ in their tolerance to the coldest temperatures of the winter, many fail to realize that temperatures that are too hot can also disturb optimal growth during the summer, or that unseasonable cold snaps might kill new growth (spring) or unhardened tissues (fall) and increase the susceptibility of a plant to stress problems. Temperature conditions that can initiate stress in a landscape plant, create a physiological dysfunction, or influence the implementation of a treatment or maintenance strategy are all relevant to the tree care professional's site inventory.

The potential for winter injury during cold temperatures is assessed during the site inventory. A professional can consult local weather bureau records as well as a ***hardiness zone map*** (available through the U.S. Department of Agriculture) to determine the expected low winter temperatures for the area in which the landscape site exists. Strong winds, bright sunshine, and low humidity will all compound some cold-related problems for landscape plants. Cold temperature damage (winter injury) to landscape plants is a particular concern whenever an introduced specimen (not native to the area) exists on the landscape. The regional adaptation of a native species is a factor of both the latitude and elevation of the site, and many times exotic, introduced plants are incapable of tolerating the same cold temperatures that do not disturb native plantings. Although nurseries are usually careful to provide adapted plant material to their clients, it is not uncommon for an arborist to find plants on site that are marginally-suited for the hardiness zone. Hardiness recommendations on new plant material selections are continuously updated by growers and university researchers. Damages related to cold temperatures vary, not only with plant species, but with age and condition of the plant. For these reasons, the plant materials inventory (previous section) and the site inventory must be used together to identify potential problems for an arborist.

While cold-adapted plants are relatively protected from cold temperatures during dormancy (after undergoing a winter-hardening process), they are particularly susceptible to low temperature stress when coming out of dormancy in the spring, or prior to assuming dormancy in the fall. Similar periods of vulnerability occur when cold temperatures resume after an unusual warm stretch in the winter. During these periods, freezing temperatures can cause extracellular or intercellular freezing which disrupts growing tissues of a plant. A site inventory will consider the incidence of freezing temperatures during the fall and winter, and consider the recent past history of the site, since the existing plants may have been affected by late spring and early fall frost or drastic temperature fluctuations.

The site inventory will, in particular, pinpoint spots within the landscape most prone to cold temperature injury, including basins or low spots on the grounds where lower temperatures may occur. Planting in these areas should be avoided; extra protection for existing plants on these sites is warranted. Grouped plantings will be better buffered from rapid temperature changes than will individual plant specimens.

The site inventory can help predict or pinpoint high temperature injuries with a recent climatic history of the site. Rapid change to hot, dry conditions following a cool, moist spring may result in high temperature damage to trees.

Light. Plants require light not only for food production (***photosynthesis***), but in order to correctly interpret seasonal changes (***photoperiod***) and control or correlate daily growth. The light conditions or ***irradiance*** available to the plants on site are related not only to the local climate, but to specifics of the existing site. For example, the presence of tall structures may shade plants, or crowded plant groupings can exclude light from some specimens. Artificial lights (decorative or security night lighting in some landscapes) may mimic or disguise the signals of the sun.

Wind. The site inventory will collect information regarding severe high winds in the recent history of the site that may have disrupted landscape plantings, but chronic prevailing winds may also be responsible for deforming plant habit. Wind is a climatic factor that has a strong influence on water loss from the leaves (through transpiration). Strong winds can help create a water deficit for a plant even when soil moisture levels would be adequate under normal conditions.

Precipitation. Precipitation records will help determine if either water deficit, or alternatively, flooding (low soil aeration) problems could have affected plants on site. The requirement of individual plants for water is closely tied to the type of planting soil (the ability of different types of soil to retain or to release moisture), and to other climatic factors (high winds or bright sunshine can, for example, increase a plant's need for water, while prolonged cloudy weather can further aggravate problems with too much water in the soil). For these reasons, the weather records can be consulted to determine both the amount of moisture added to the soil, and the likely level of water use by the plants (transpiration). Other moisture-related conditions such as fog or relative humidity also influence the amount of moisture actually made available to a plant, and its reaction to other climatic factors.

Urban stress. Developed sites have unique climatic conditions that impact on the health and performance of the landscape plants. In general, the buffering effects of grouped plants are reduced, as solitary specimens are more often placed in limited planting spaces. This problem increases the susceptibility of a plant to rapid temperature change. Pavement placed around plantings in an urban setting also increase site temperatures, and city structures change wind and radiation patterns around the plants. Coincident with urban sites are problems with salt damage and with pollution. Deicing salts tend to accumulate around plant root systems. Air quality may be poor not only for an urban planting site, but for any site in the prevailing wind direction from a factory emitting pollutants. Chemical injuries may occur on non-targeted plants as a side effect of herbicides used to control weeds on a landscape site.

> *The site inventory will pinpoint spots within the landscape most prone to cold temperature injury.*

> *Developed urban sites have unique climatic conditions that impact on the health and performance of landscape plants.*

> *Each soil characteristic is directly related to the water available to the plant through the root system and the nutrition the plant has to utilize for growth.*

SITE FACTORS: SOIL

Soil texture (particle size), structure (degree of **particle aggregation**) and aerated depth all influence plant growth on a planting site. Each soil characteristic is directly related to the water available to the plant through the root system, oxygen available in the soil atmosphere, and the essential elements the plant has to utilize for growth. The site inventory will record these facts as well as any information about slopes or inclinations on the landscape site, and soil fertility, soil pH and soil strength.

The site inventory record of soil texture (particle size) will determine the relative composition and proportions of clay, silt, or sand particles on a landscape. Clay particles are the smallest, waferlike particles with high surface area ratios and water holding capacities; sand particles are the largest, more blocky or spherical in shape, and don't retain much water. Silt particles fall between the two in size. Loam soils have intermediate characteristics because they combine different types of soil particles, and therefore have a combination of soil properties. The structure (presence and size of **aeration pores**) is determined by how much these soil particles are aggregated together. When aggregates are compressed (by traffic or construction, for example), normal soil structure may be destroyed by compaction. **Compaction damage** is most severe when soils are wet. The depth of the aerated soil gives a clue to how far a plant's root system extends, and therefore can help predict plant tolerance to drought.

Soil on a typical urban site may vary widely across a property and several samples may need to be taken. Soil analysis of samples is generally available through soil testing services or university services to aid in determining some of these soil specifics. The status of the soil on a planting site can also be assessed by knowing the history of the planting area. If a site was stripped of valuable topsoil during construction, or if different soil (unlike the native soil surrounding the site) was used to replace soil, the planting site will have lost much of the useful properties needed for optimal plant growth.

Soil topography (presence of slopes and level areas) is an important record for the site inventory, as topographical variety presents additional challenges for management. Mounds or sloped areas are effective to provide surface drainage, but problems with erosion or waterlogging at the gully of a slope can be serious site problems.

Chemical properties of the soil include reaction (**pH**) which controls the availability of many required **macro** and **microelements**. It is important to know the soil pH prior to fertility treatments. Soils of different textures vary widely in mineral and nutrient content, and ability to release these to growing plant roots.

SITE FACTORS: INJURY AND STRESS

Site inventory will give the PHC practitioner an edge in predicting, diagnosing, or preventing a wide variety of physiological dysfunctions that results when climate or soil are unfavorable for woody plant growth. Many plant symptoms which would be extremely difficult to diagnose immediately can be predicted or identified easily with a site record in hand. For example, cold temperatures during midwinter can cause **dehydration damage**, which occurs when water is forced out of plant cells. For broadleaf evergreens and some conifers, this injury will create discoloration or browning of foliage. Another low temperature injury related to dehydration occurs when wood cells are physically split apart (called **frost cracking**, although the term is somewhat misleading). Rapid drops in temperature, or shading of sun-warmed tissues can cause serious disruption of cells, killing evergreen foliage or creating dead patches of bark

> *Many plant symptoms can be predicted or identified easily with a site record in hand.*

SITE INFORMATION CHECKLIST

Incidence of site conditions

Low temperatures (extremes encountered on site)

Rapid temperature loss/change:

High temperatures (extremes encountered on site):

Irradiance:

Wind:

Precipitation:

Urban conditions
- pollution:
- salt or chemical injuries:

Soil factors — on various locations in landscape
- soil type:
  — texture:
  — structure:
  — depth:
  — pH:
  — fertility:
  — salts:
  — compaction:
  — organic matter
  — water drainage
  — water availability
- topography:

Soil cover/turf or other cover:

Related injuries or problems (record calendar date(s) of unusual/severe climate change)

Influence on maintenance practices:

Procedures to modify the condition:

Key stress identification:

Figure 7 - 5. Example of a *Site Information Checklist*.

(cankers) on a tree. Winter kill of flower buds, twig dieback and defoliation can all relate to past temperature conditions on a site. Unsuitable high temperatures can injure plants by desiccation, when water loss from the leaves exceeds the ability of the roots to resupply water.

Inability of densely-shaded, crowded plantings to intercept adequate light may account for observed defoliation problems, pale foliage color, or the spindly, "leggy" appearance of some specimens on a site. Similarly, plants that have been sheared routinely tend to suffer from lack of light penetration within the dense outer shell of the shrub or tree, and therefore may in fact become weak and susceptible to damage. Trees that are lighted artificially may fail to assume normal fall color, or go into dormancy at the proper time, therefore may become more susceptible to cold temperature injuries. ***Dieback*** might occur just on a few branches or on one side of a tree, if only part of the plant is close to the artificial lights. Severe wind damage may be evidenced by broken plant branches or plants partially uprooted from the soil. ***Wilting*** is a symptom caused by wind combined with water deficit conditions. Plants suffering water deficits tend to drop foliage or plant parts (usually older tissues first).

Salinity problems on plants can show up as leaf scorching, bud drop, and dieback. In general, the plant growth rate is severely and obviously stunted. ***Pollution damage*** causes mostly foliar symptoms, which vary with the type of pollutant affecting the site. Soil that is heavy (for example, a fine clay soil) will contribute to drainage problems around a plant and compound damages caused by flooded conditions. Coarse planting soil may not provide adequate water retention, and consequently, the plants will be more susceptible to wilting due to water deficits.

SITE FACTORS: MAINTENANCE

Unfavorable climatic conditions for landscape plants can be alleviated in part by a tree care professional's planned maintenance procedures. The maintenance practices available to the arborist to counteract or avoid expected site problems are varied and numerous. For example, problems induced by water deficit (drought), which might normally increase the susceptibility of a tree to attack by an insect pest, can be circumvented through timely irrigation. Irrigation may counteract potential cold temperature desiccation and improve the heat absorption and transmission of the surrounding soil. Shading, or mass planting (grouping) of plant materials can be useful practices for avoiding damage from rapid temperature changes. In order to avoid frost injury, practices that slow down plant growth (reduction in fertilization or irrigation, for example) help encourage hardening. Site selection to avoid frost pockets may include using landscape structures (concrete walls, for example) near the planting to provide protection. Mulching around the base of the tree can partially compensate for inadequate soil structure (aid in drainage) and buffer soil temperatures around the surface roots of a tree.

Careful selective, feathered pruning of plants, in lieu of shearing of hedges or pollarding trees, is a maintenance step that improves the light intercepted by a plant, and the aeration throughout the canopy. Pruning and training steps (when improperly done) can compound light-interception stress to a plant, while professional pruning and training maximizes light available to each plant. As an additional bonus, properly-pruned and maintained plants become more resistant to other stress problems, once the severe pruning stress is alleviated.

Timely and proper irrigation scheduling can be planned following site inventory of factors related to available moisture. Irrigation (leaching) is also a primary maintenance step to control existing urban soil salinity problems, combined with measures (shielding, for example) that will avoid further salt conta-

> *Unfavorable climatic conditions for landscape plants can be alleviated in part by tree care professionals.*

> *Timely and proper irrigation scheduling can be planned following site inventory of factors related to available moisture.*

mination. When flooded conditions, compounded by heavy compacted soil structure, are in evidence, sometimes the only available techniques for the PHC practitioner may be plant removal or expensive drainage installation, soil rejuvenation (breaking up, amending, and regrading), or soil terracing steps. Steps to avoid compaction damage (scheduling work only when soil is dry and rerouting traffic) should be practiced routinely.

Plant protection from wind or light damage may be warranted maintenance procedures. Wind damage detected on a site might be prevented in later years by grouping plants into mass plantings, or installing landscape structures that block the wind and afford some protection. Landscape plants (or individual sections of a tree) that fail to go into normal dormancy in the fall may need to be shielded from security lights.

For problems with heavy soils (inadequate drainage or water movement), the professional can modify a site by using raised planters or mounds to increase surface drainage. This practice also effectively increases soil depth. Soil reaction can be adjusted chemically via addition of lime (to increase pH) or a sulfur compound (to decrease pH). Accurate, rugged, pocket-sized portable pH meters (glass electrode models) are available to detect soil pH, and determine nutrient availability. Irrigation scheduling is tied to soil characteristics on site, as well as planned soil fertilization steps (how much fertilizer to apply, and with which fertilizer formulation to supplement). Mulching is an excellent procedure for improving limited soil conditions. Mulch can be applied in cases of hard, heavy, compacted soils to allow surface root formation that would otherwise be precluded, and mulch can compensate in part for inadequate rooting depth. A mulched soil surface can further improve infiltration of water and prevent runoff on inadequate soils. These potential cultural management strategies are discussed in more detail in Chapter 9.

PREPARING A LANDSCAPE MAP

Preparing a landscape map of a property is a process that integrates all of the inventory information (species identifications), special notations for key plants, site specifics (Figure 7-5), and other information about the plants [size, location on the property, condition] (Figure 7-4). This information is consolidated into a useful, visually-descriptive, coordinated master plan — the landscape map (Figure 7-6). The monitor will prepare this basic working document, which will be consulted prior to beginning planned maintenance, including any services conducted as part of a PHC program.

A landscape map should include enough details to be useful in practice...

A landscape map should include enough details to be useful in practice, and should be drawn to sufficient scale for maximizing its utility as a decision-making tool. The map should contain sufficient detail to provide an adequate reference for consultation between the PHC practitioner and client. This will leave no question or confusion concerning exactly which specimens on a site are targeted for removal or treatment, or which locations are being considered for replanting. The map includes a scaled layout of all structures (buildings, patios, drives or walkways) on site, and a diagram of the entire size and shape of the property.

Next, each of the plants on site are individually drawn on the map, to pinpoint their location. The routine method used by landscape designers to symbolically represent trees on a site (Figure 7-6) also gives a bird's-eye view of the spread of each tree. Grouped plantings, or plants arranged in a hedge, are represented in the map to reflect as accurately as possible the actual layout of plants on the property.

80 / **THE PLANT HEALTH CARE MANAGEMENT SYSTEM**

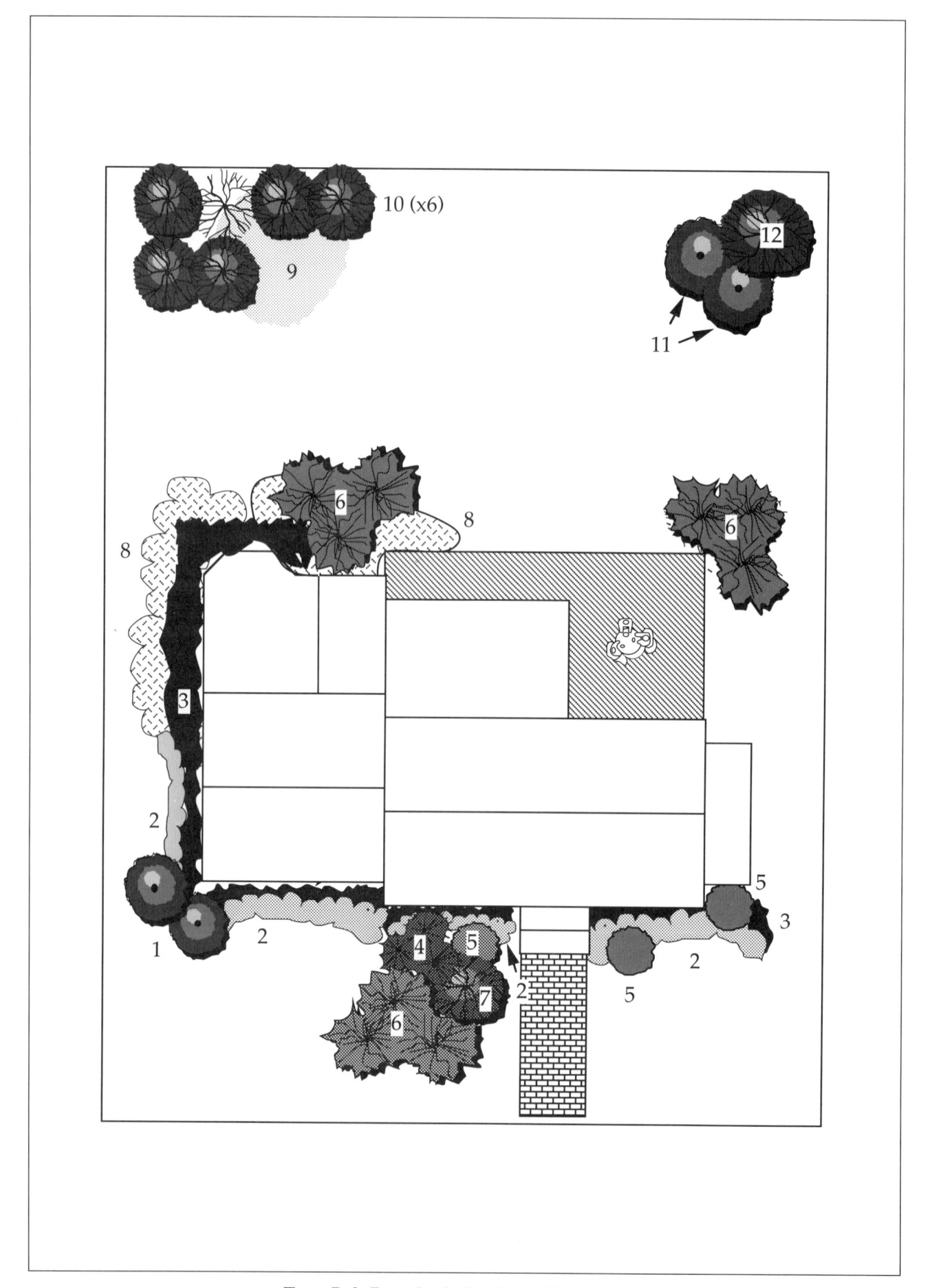

Figure 7-6. Example of a *Landscape Map.*

> *The scientific name, in addition to a common name for the species, should be included on the site map.*

Especially for densely-planted properties, specimens can be labeled with numbers on the map. The species designation for each plant, and other relevant information (below) can be included in a separate legend to the side of the actual map, to minimize confusion (or, the species list for an individual property as shown in Figure 7-4 can include the species code and number designation keyed to an attached landscape map). As was described for the species identification section above, the scientific name, in addition to a common name, should be included on the site map. If the specimen in question is a key plant (a plant likely to require repeated intensive maintenance because it is prone to stress, as described in an earlier section), it should be designated with a special symbol or notation to alert both the PHC professional and the client to the need for special consideration for the plant.

Three other items of information regarding the size, condition and location of each plant on the site are required to complete the map designations. Each of these additional items are relevant to the actual landscape value of a specimen, and are therefore crucial to making decisions regarding treatment options, or possible removal or relocation of trees and shrubs.

Size. While the landscape map will symbolically illustrate the spread of the landscape specimen, additional information about size (which relates to the age) is needed to determine value and importance of an individual plant in the landscape. Shrubs are placed in a size category based on both height and spread. Tree trunk diameter is obtained using special calipers or measuring tools using the following criteria:

- For trunks under 4-inches, measure the diameter 6-inches above the ground.
- For trunks 4- to 8-inches in diameter, measure diameter 12-inches above the ground.
- For trunks larger than 8-inches in diameter, measure diameter 4.5-feet above the ground (along the trunk axis, not DBH).
- For multi-stemmed trees or tight clump of several trees where each contributes its proportionate share to the canopy, measure each trunk according to the above and add the diameters together.

For trees, in general, the larger the size and maturity of the specimen, the more valuable it becomes to the landscape site. A very large elegant specimen shade tree may warrant expensive or time-intensive maintenance (for example, cabling of weak limbs) in a client's landscape, whereas the value of similar treatments for a smaller tree might be questionable. The size designation recorded at the initial time of map development can be updated easily during subsequent years of maintaining a client's property.

Condition. The condition of each plant at the time of initial map construction can be recorded (e.g. degree of disease damage, percentage of defoliation, presence of damaged limbs). With continued, regular maintenance on each plant, the PHC manager can upgrade the condition classification, and at the same time effectively illustrate the beneficial influence of the PHC strategy on value enhancement for the site.

Location. The location classification is not just the actual physical location of a plant on a site (as designated on a map in terms of distance from a property border or a building), but considers the importance of a plant on that part of the site to the complete landscape. For example, large shade trees which effectively frame an entranceway to a home have a more important location than the same trees located in a grouping of other trees on a less prominent part of the property. The location is a critical factor especially in terms of considered plant removals or replanting decisions. Location includes specific site, contribution and placement components.

Each of these relevant information items—species, size, condition, and location—can be inserted into a formula which has been designed to calculate the inherent value of a specimen to the site. For specific directions on how to construct a valuation equation, see the *Guide for Plant Appraisal, Eighth Edition* published by the International Society of Arboriculture. This reference also provides more detailed information about how to numerically use species, size, location, and condition factors for each specimen, to aid in the final valuation calculation. The value assessment is a tangible tool that helps to emphasize the actual monetary worth of healthy, well-maintained landscape plants to the client. The valuation calculation provides a clear illustration on how an arborist's professional maintenance (as reflected in the condition classification of the valuation formula) will enhance property value over time, and can help gauge the merit of alternative treatment strategies for the overall landscape.

> *The landscape map gives the arborist a template, for marking areas needing action.*

The landscape map gives the arborist a template, during subsequent monitoring on the site, for marking areas needing action. The basic (master copy) of the map can be annotated to point out problems that have been noted during monitoring, and to alert as to the need for subsequent action. Computer-aided preparation of the map is an excellent method, when practical, as a computer file of a map can most easily be manipulated to access inventory information and locational data, modified to reflect new plantings, removals, or tree growth for long-term clients, and consulted to determine progress evaluations. As an example, AutoCAD (a general purpose computer-aided design program) and the landscape-specific LandCAD, are used to prepare municipal tree maps to aid in the planning process and efficiency of maintenance; other commercial arboriculture firms offer similar services including computer-aided map preparation and inventory records. Recommendations and alternatives for planned maintenance can be noted directly on the landscape map. The map can, therefore, be an effective, illustrative tool for discussion with the client or instruction with the working crew.

CHAPTER SUMMARY

The steps taken to develop a landscape plant inventory include:

- *Identifying woody plants:*
  — Seek training in woody plant identification skills;
  — obtain good reference identification manuals for your geographical area;
  — learn to recognize characteristic morphological features of plants and use these to distinguish individual species.

- *Using the key plant/key stress strategy:*
  — Target the key plants/key stress that have the potential for recurrent problems in your geographic area;
  — identify any key plants on a specific landscape site, and plan for maintenance and management based on expected stress problems;
  — capitalize on PHC successes with key plants/key stress to build support for a holistic PHC program for an entire landscape or business operation;
  — whenever possible, design new landscapes or suggest plant replacements excluding these problem-prone plant species.
- *Recording site specific features and problems:*
  — Include an assessment of all climatic and soil features which are likely to influence the performance and health of plants on the landscape site.

— Alleviate undesirable site problems via planned maintenance, and consult the site inventory as a guideline during routine maintenance.

- *Mapping relevant information about the landscape:*
  — Combine information about species identification, key plants/key stress alert, and site specifics with additional data about the plants on a sufficiently scaled, detailed visual plan which can be consulted prior to any future on-site maintenance.

CHAPTER 8

PHC Diagnosis

INTRODUCTION

> *To be a good diagnostician, you must be a good botanist, that is, you must know what a healthy plant looks like...*

Correct diagnosis of plant problems is the keystone to PHC. Improper diagnosis leads to improper treatment which at best is wasteful and at worst, delays correct actions, often making the problem more difficult or impossible to solve. Diagnosis is the process of determining the identity or cause of a stress problem. Before the process can begin, you must first recognize a problem exists.

To be a good diagnostician, you must be a good botanist, that is, you must know what a healthy plant looks like, its internal structure, and the proper functioning of each of the plant parts. A healthy plant must grow, respond to external stimulants, and reproduce. Each plant part contributes to the successful accomplishment of these activities. A good diagnostician will know:

- the different tissues in the leaf blade and how each functions to obtain maximum food production (*photosynthesis*)
- the different tissues of the terminal and lateral buds on stems and how each functions to obtain maximum twig growth
- the different tissues of flowers and fruit and how each functions to obtain maximum reproduction by the parent plant
- the different tissues of the stems, branches, and trunks and how they provide stability, increase in diameter and utilize the ***xylem*** and ***phloem*** to transport water, elements, and ***photosynthate*** to all living cells.
- the different tissues of the roots and how they absorb water and essential elements, transport them to the trunk, and anchor the tree framework solidly in the ground.
- the different tissues of the tree that function to conserve and defend food, food storage space, and respire.

A healthy plant can exist only in a suitable environment. A good diagnostician will know and understand the light, air, water, and soil requirements for plants. Light is the energy source for photosynthesis. Most plants grow best in full sun while others tolerate or prefer partial shade. Day length governs the functioning of some plant activities. Air provides the carbon dioxide needed for photosynthesis and the oxygen used in respiration. Air must be present in the soil as well as above ground. Hopefully the air will have a suitable range of temperatures and will contain no pollutants.

Living plant cells are primarily filled with water. This is usually obtained from soil. ***Capillary water*** is available to absorbing roots while ***hygroscopic*** and ***gravitational water*** is not. The soil and its organic matter must supply a continuing source of plant elements. Soil pH determines the availability of several of the elements to roots.

The activities and the preferences of humans have created environmental conditions that are not optimum for tree growth. In evolutionary terms, urbanization is a recent development. Humans have been crowded into cities for less that 10,000 years. The evolution of tree genera and species required millions of years. Trees that we accept as desirable horticulturally and aesthetically are taken from an environment to which they have naturally adapted and placed in one in which the soil and ambient conditions are radically altered. Stress is therefore a constant condition for urban trees.

DIAGNOSIS OF PLANT DISEASES AND INSECT PROBLEMS

> *A plant disease is defined as an abnormal plant condition resulting from the activity of a causal agent over time that disrupts the normal physiology of the plant and results in visual symptoms.*

A plant stress problem can be defined as an abnormal plant condition resulting from the activity of a **causal agent** that, over time, disrupts the normal physiology of the plant and results in visual symptoms. The causal agent can be living, e.g., fungus, virus, mycoplasma-like organism (MLO), bacterium, etc.; or non-living, e.g., environmental or climatic changes. Diseases are distinguished from injuries. Injuries have a causal agent, but occur in a short period of time, e.g., seconds, minutes, days. The prolonged presence of parasitic insects and mites is technically a disease, but generally is considered an injury. Diseases that are caused by living causal agents are **infectious**, that is, they can be transmitted from diseased to healthy plants. Non-living causal agents initiate tree reactions that we term stress.

Non-living agents cause more damage to amenity plants (plants that are retained in the landscape to please or serve the function of people) than do all insects and infectious agents combined. Non-living stress causal agents are difficult to diagnose because the causal agent has no body or form, they leave no by-products, and often mimic infectious disease symptoms.

The process used by the diagnostician to determine that a problem exists and its severity will vary with individuals. A procedure used by many includes the following steps:

1. The problem plant is given a cursory or superficial examination. If all the bark is removed from the trunk, or a known destructive insect or disease organism is present, no further steps are necessary — diagnosis was easy. Unfortunately, this is usually not the case and we must proceed further.
2. Examine nearby plants of the same species. Do they look the same as the plant in question?
3. Examine all nearby plants. Are they abnormal? Do the features resemble those of the plant in question?
4. Determine precisely the species of the problem plant. Texts listing commonly occurring insects and diseases on that species in your area are usually available.
5. Determine the history of the plant and site. Ask about cultural practices and weather conditions. Remember that the client rarely has adequate records or total recall.
6. Examine the entire plant thoroughly. Especially note annual twig growth; leaf size, coloration and distortion; insect skeletons, frass, eggs or feces; fungal fruiting bodies; and leaf, stem, trunk and root abnormalities.
7. When an infectious disease is suspected that can only, or best, be confirmed by laboratory analysis, take an appropriate sample for testing.

In diagnosing tree problems we usually place observations into categories. An initial division often is symptoms and signs. **Symptoms** are the result of physiological disturbances and are evident as plant reactions to environmental changes. **Signs** are structures of a causal agent or highly characteristic tree reactions that persist on the plant. The presence of signs along with typical symptoms can make diagnosis an easy procedure. Unfortunately, signs are not present with many infectious agents and are never present with non-living stress causal agents. We then must rely on symptoms and plant history.

Similar symptoms expressed by diseased plants can often result from the activity of different pathogens. The usual procedure by the diagnostician is to eliminate as many causes as possible before closely examining the evidence to determine which of the remaining possibilities is, or is likely, the causal agent. The problem becomes even more complex when two or more agents are involved.

In a following section, symptoms from four major categories will be described: (1) selection, site and planting problems, (2) problems arising from plant maintenance, (3) diseases, and (4) insect and mite damage. As will become evident, many cause the same symptoms. Environmental stress can result in more severe decline than would normally be observed.

TOOLS FOR DIAGNOSIS

> *A correct diagnosis of tree troubles is based on observations of the injured or sick tree and the surrounding healthy trees.*

A correct diagnosis of tree troubles is based on observations of the injured or sick tree and the surrounding healthy trees. Roots, stems and leaves must be examined. Tree characteristics are more readily obtained when the diagnostician has several tools available for field use. Proper equipment makes the job easier, faster, and more complete. Some tools are required at almost every site and other tools can be useful under special conditions or for special purposes. Hand pruners, a knife, a hand axe, extension pruners, a saw, a shovel, and a hand lens or magnifying glass are essential.

An *increment hammer* or *increment borer*, soil auger or *soil profile tube*, diameter tape, binoculars, a hammer along with a punch or gouge, camera, compass, pH meter, gas detector, soil moisture meter, plastic bags and glass vials are very useful additions to the diagnostic kit.

ESSENTIAL TOOLS

Hand pruners or **shears** are used to obtain leaf, twig or branch specimens for closer examination of insect or disease problems. Branch specimens can be obtained suitable for *laboratory culturing* of *systemic disease* organisms. These are usually 6 inches in length and 1/2 to 3/4 inches in diameter. A smooth cut across the end of the branch sample will reveal the presence of discoloration in the outer sapwood or inner heartwood.

A **knife** is useful in detecting certain diseases and insect injuries. Cankers not readily visible in the outer bark become evident when the bark is shaved away. Fruiting bodies of fungal pathogens can be seen as black, pinhead sized circles with white centers. Dead twigs can be notched back to living tissue and the margin between the two observed. The sizes of cankers can be determined. Borer injury can be distinguished from other injuries. Insects can be found in many of the leaf galls.

A **hand axe** or **hatchet** serves much like a knife, being used on larger twigs or branches. It also can be used to remove chips from trunks for laboratory culturing and bark from wood to determine color and odor of inner phloem. Tapping the bark with a knife or hatchet can reveal the hollow sound of loose, dead bark. This tool can cause damage and should be used only when a punch won't suffice.

An **extension pruner** saves the time and labor of climbing trees to collect twigs and leaves above the diagnostician's reach. It serves much the same purpose as hand pruners and saws. Even when climbing is necessary to reach the problem area, extension pruners can more safely reach the ends of branches without the need for walking on or being supported by branches too small to support the climber's weight.

A **saw** is required when the branch or root sample desired is too large to cut with a knife or shears. Injuries, insects and disease organisms often are found on/in trunks and large branches that can only be severed with a saw.

A **tile spade** is the tool commonly used to determine the condition of the soil or to obtain root samples for observation or laboratory culturing. Girdling roots, basal cankers, root rots, and air inadequate for root system use can be determined by removing soil from the base of a tree. Soil texture, compaction, moisture content, and topsoil depth are evident by trenching to a depth of at least 24 inches to observe profile.

Many tree insect and disease problems become more evident when magnified with a 6- to 10-power **hand lens**. Mechanical injury can often be distinguished from insect injury and infectious disease distinguished from physiological problems. Mites, aphids, and other small insects can be identified with more certainty after magnification. The widths of a tree's annual growth increments are much more easily established.

SPECIAL FUNCTION TOOLS

An **increment hammer** or **increment borer** removes a small cylindrical core of bark and wood from the tree. Wood cores are useful in determining a general decline in annual wood production through the last few years.

A **soil auger** or **soil profile tube** removes a core of soil from the ground. It is less destructive to use in turf areas than a shovel. Soil samples can be easily collected from several areas for soil tests. A profile tube allows the undisturbed soil profile to be examined.

A **diameter tape** is calibrated in such a manner that diameter is precisely determined when the tape is placed around the circumference of a tree trunk.

Binoculars or **field glasses** aid in determining the condition of leaves or twigs in tall trees. The extent of dying branches can be established. Often scale insect infestation can be diagnosed.

A **gouge** or **punch** such as a leather punch can be hammered through the bark and small, mostly inconspicuous, circles of bark removed to determine inner phloem color and smell. Bark diseases and cambium inhibiting borer insects can be detected. The small holes created rapidly close with callus in healthy trees.

Photographs can record the progression of damage over time, or be taken to specialists to aid in describing an unknown problem.

pH meters determine the soil acidity or alkalinity. Alkaline soils are especially unsuitable because of the lack of availability of certain essential nutrients and the accompanying chlorosis.

Gas detectors determine the presence of undesirable gasses in the soil. These gasses displace oxygen that is essential for root health and growth.

Soil moisture content can roughly be determined by sifting soil through your fingers, but is much more precisely determined with a **moisture meter**.

Plastic bags and **glass vials** are useful in the collection of specimen leaves and twigs for laboratory culturing or the collection of specimen insects.

> *Many tree insect and disease problems become more evident when magnified with a hand lens.*

DIAGNOSIS CHECKLIST

SEQUENCE OF STEPS IN DIAGNOSIS:

1. Superficial examination
   Symptoms/Signs?
2. Examination of neighboring plants
3. Determine plant species
4. Acquire site and plant history
5. Thorough plant examination
6. Laboratory confirmation/analysis
7. Holistic summary and establishment of the site and plant context for prescribing treatments.

Proper use of these tools will assist in the efficient diagnosis of tree problems. Only after correct diagnosis can the proper treatment be recommended or applied.

SITING, SELECTING, AND PLANTING PROBLEMS

> *Many tree troubles arise because the "right plant was not planted in the right place."*

Many tree troubles arise because the "right plant was not planted in the right place." Under these conditions the selected plant will suffer environmental stress from the initial placement in the ground. The primary subjects to be examined when young trees do not perform as desired are soil, site, climate and planting technique. The symptoms expressed by the plant may not be definitive, but they will be indicative. The symptoms will direct attention to factors where additional examination or study will lead to a satisfactory diagnosis.

Soil. The soil present at the planting site can limit plant success. In their natural environment tree roots grow in topsoil. This is often 10-15 inches deep, is well drained, and contains the mineral elements, air, water and organic matter required for adequate growth of trees. In urban sites, the topsoil often has been disturbed and frequently is shallow, compacted and subject to drought. Under these conditions trees are continuously under stress. Leaves will be small and pale and annual twig growth will be short.

The physical aspects of the soil are more important than the chemical aspects. The physical aspects include *soil texture*, *soil structure*, *profile*, *compaction* and *water holding capacity*. The texture of soil is determined by the size of its particles. Soil is formed from rock that has weathered for thousands of years. The weathering results in some particles being very small (clay), others somewhat larger (silt), and others larger still (sand). The percentage of each of these in combination determines soil texture. Texture is a major factor in establishing water holding capacity of soil.

Sandy soils have large pore spaces and retain the least amount of water. Plants in sandy soils are quite subject to drought. Clayey soils have small pore spaces and retain the most amount of water. Under optimum conditions, soil should be 50% mineral and 50% pore space. Pore space should be 50% air and 50% water for best plant growth. Both oxygen and water are essential for root growth. Plants in clayey soils are more subject to flooding injury (oxygen starvation).

Silty soils are intermediate in pore space size and when combined with some sand and some clay (called loams) are best suited for plant growth and depending on the hydrology of the site, may be the least subject to **drought** or **flooding stress**. Compaction of silt or clay soils further decreases pore space and increases environmental stress. Compaction of soils by equipment or animals is more severe when soils are wet. Trees should not be planted in compacted soils.

The chemical aspects of soil include the available elements, soil pH, and soil organic matter content. Most soils contain all of the nutrients essential for plant growth. Nitrogen is the **macroelement** most likely to limit growth. Soil pH (acidic, alkalinic) is a governing factor in nutrient availability. A pH of 6.0 to 6.5 is optimum for most trees and shrubs. A pH above 7 (alkaline) often limits the availability of certain micronutrients (iron, manganese, zinc) and can result in chlorotic (yellow), slow growing plants. Soil contains living organisms (earthworms, fungi, bacteria). Over the centuries they produce persisting organic matter in soils. **Organic matter** is beneficial in improving soil structure, nutrient exchange, and water holding capacity. Soil tests will determine nutrient content, organic matter content, and soil pH. Results from soil tests frequently aid in diagnosing *environmental stress* caused by soil factors.

Site. The location where the newly planted trees are placed can also govern environmental stress effects on young trees. Site factors include plant spacing, plant size and the presence of streets, buildings and utilities. Trees are living organisms that grow larger each year. Even heavily pruned bonsai trees increase in size. Plants require sunlight for production of food materials. Most woody plants require full sunlight for proper growth and bloom, but some will do well in light shade. Few tree species perform well in dense shade.

Each plant needs an adequate growing space. Space in the soil is required for the roots to obtain water, oxygen and nutrients and space in the air for the crown to obtain carbon dioxide, oxygen and sunlight. Plants compete for each of these elements. Competition results in environmental stress when one or more element is limited. The most common error made by laymen is to plant too many trees or shrubs in a limited space.

Perennial plants require more space each year as they grow larger. Selection of plant material that does not take into account ultimate mature height, crown width, and rooting space results in excessive plant competition and decline and death of the more stressed plants.

Buildings, streets, sidewalks and utilities can restrict and alter the growing space of trees. Building foundations, streets, and sidewalks often are constructed of alkaline materials which change soil pH. Buildings and streets reflect light and heat and create unsuitable growing conditions for twigs and leaves. Artificial light from street lighting may change the natural dormant growing season rhythms of trees and result in winter injury. Sidewalks, streets and parking lots restrict the quantity of rainfall entering the soil and may result in drought conditions. Removal of major roots during construction or repair of underground utilities can cause decline in tree crowns. These site factors and others must be considered in the diagnosis of environmental stress problems in trees.

Climate. Plants often are selected for planting that are not adapted to the area. When the genetic composition of the plant requires specific temperature and moisture conditions and these are not present at the planting site, the plant will decline and die. Temperature and moisture conditions appropriate for ade-

> *The location where the newly planted trees are placed can govern environmental stress effects on young trees.*

quate growth are often lumped into the term ***plant hardiness***. The ability to withstand low temperatures in winter is a major component of plant hardiness. Amount of rainfall and distribution of rainfall during the growing season will also influence plant hardiness. Nursery catalogs and Extension Service circulars often give the zones of plant hardiness for each of the trees and shrubs listed.

Unusual or untimely, extreme weather conditions can cause damage to hardy plants. Low temperatures in the spring after shoot emergence can kill young shoots on evergreens. Very low temperatures in winter can open freeze cracks on the trunks of trees. Alternating periods of warm and freezing temperatures in winter are the primary cause of winter injury on woody plants. Most woody plants can survive flooding for a few days but some may be killed when the roots remain beneath water for a week or more. Droughts result in root death and droughts for two or more years can result in twig dieback and decline on most woody plants.

Improper planting. Plants with inadequate root systems or plants improperly placed in the ground will often die. Laymen are often puzzled when plants survive the first year but die the season following transplanting. Woody plants often have ***stored reserves*** sufficient to maintain life for one year but rarely enough for two. When the root system does not become established well enough the first year to provide at least a maintenance requirement of water and nutrients, plants die. A wide hole of the correct depth with suitable backfill and proper supplemental watering will encourage root regeneration. Avoid potholes in clay soils that have inadequate drainage. Avoid girdling roots and girdling wires. A good diagnostician always asks when the tree was planted and what were the follow-up procedures.

PROBLEMS ARISING FROM MAINTENANCE

> *Maintenance problems include chemical injury, construction injury, mechanical injury, injury from animals, or combinations of these.*

Maintenance problems include chemical injury, construction injury, mechanical injury, injury from animals, or combinations of these. The extent of dieback and decline resulting from these injuries depend on how much of the injured plant part was destroyed. The most common injury to trees and shrubs results from misapplication of pesticides, especially the herbicides used extensively to kill weeds or weed seedlings in lawns. Herbicides especially formulated to kill broad-leaved weeds also can kill or severely injure deciduous and evergreen trees. Warnings on pesticide labels state where and when the product can be safely applied to the target plant. Misapplication, drift, or vaporization of the herbicide may place the herbicide on non-target plants and result in chemical injury. When distortion, cupping or unnatural shapes of leaves are encountered, herbicide injury should be a suspect candidate.

Sterilants used to maintain clear soil at the base of fences are mobile and persistent in soil. They kill tree and shrub roots present in the treated area. Some of these materials are even mobile in plants. These kill elongated strips of bark extending up from the treated root or may kill entire plants. Death of plant parts from misapplication of fungicides and insecticides is much less likely. Leaf spotting or leaf defoliation can occur when label instructions are not followed. Salt applied as a deicing agent can injure plant roots, but is especially serious as drift on evergreen plants down-wind from streets or highways. Air pollution is not a major cause of plant decline except in limited, defined areas. Plant death can occur near sources of sulfur and fluoride pollutants. Ozone rarely causes more than a pale mottling of plant leaves, but may predispose plants to decline.

> *Roots of trees and shrubs grow best in those areas where moisture, nutrients, and oxygen are optimum.*

Construction injury is a common cause of tree death. The injury can result from soil cuts, soil fills, and/or soil compaction. Roots of trees and shrubs grow best in those areas where moisture, nutrients, and oxygen are optimum. This may be at distances much greater than branch spread. Roots will likely not be uniformly distributed beneath the tree branches. Since at present there are not readily available methods to determine where plant roots are located, the amount of decline that will result from specific acts during construction cannot be predicted. Trenches near trees sever major tree roots. Reduction in root capacity beyond 50% is likely to result in crown dieback. Removal of topsoil beneath trees removes the non-woody roots of trees. Removal of more than 2 inches of soil over tree roots can result in branch decline throughout the tree crown. Addition of soil over tree roots can hinder the soil's *water:oxygen balance*. Some tree species can adapt to this fill situation more readily than others. White oaks are easily killed when subjected to 2 or more inches of soil fill. Compaction of soil acts on roots much as does soil fills; the availability of water and oxygen is altered. Trees that die or severely decline within 2 to 5 years after home, street or driveway construction probably suffer from construction injury.

Mechanical injury can result from many human causes other than construction; string trimmers, lawnmowers, automobiles, flower bed formation, and tree injections are but a few. When insects, disease organisms, and chemical implants are not complicating factors, the extent of decline to be expected from mechanical injury is related to the amount of girdling that occurred around the plant stem. When over 50% of the bark is removed from the circumference, crown decline can be expected. Tree wounds made for purposes of injection are a relatively small portion of tree circumference, but toxicity from the injected chemical can increase tree girdling considerably. Disease organisms that enter through wounds may cause cankers or may kill susceptible trees. Boring insects are more likely to infest wound-stressed trees.

Injury by animals. Animals other than man can injure trees and shrubs. Deer, squirrels and rodents feed on twigs or bark during winter. Mulch around tree trunks can mask basal stem injury by rodents. (Mulch against the trunk also encourages the entrance of pathogenic fungi.) Certain birds (sapsuckers) feed on sap and create holes through the bark in order to obtain it. Sapsucker injury appears as several rows of small holes completely around the main stem of favored trees. Insect injury can be both mechanical and chemical. Typical damage from insects and related animals is discussed later in this chapter.

DISEASES

Diseases of trees and shrubs can be categorized by type of pathogen or by type of injury. Since the diagnostician is most involved with signs or symptoms on plant parts, diseases will be very briefly described as leaf diseases on deciduous trees, leaf diseases on evergreens, leaf and twig diseases, stem and root diseases, and systemic diseases. Textbooks and reference books are available for more detailed information.

LEAF DISEASES ON DECIDUOUS TREES
All shade trees are attacked by one or more pathogens that cause leaf diseases. The common names of these diseases are often based on the symptoms caused, the extent of injury, or the type of pathogen present.

- Scattered, rather definite, oval, angular or irregularly shaped dead areas are called **leaf spots**.

> *All shade trees are attacked by one or more pathogens that cause leaf diseases.*

- When major portions of the leaf blade are dead, the disease is a **blotch**.
- When entire leaves are killed, the disease is a **blight**.
- **Scab** is a roughened, crust-like diseased area on the surface of a leaf or fruit.
- **Rusts** are lesions with golden-yellow to reddish brown coloration and powdery texture.
- **Powdery mildews** are pathogenic fungi mostly on the surface that give leaves a light grayish, powdery appearance.
- **Sooty molds** are fungi that live on honeydew secreted by insects on the leaf surface and form a sooty coating.
- **Leaf blisters** are raised, wrinkled, blistered areas on the upper leaf surface.
- **Anthracnose** diseases are not based on symptoms, but on the group of fungi that cause them. Anthracnose disease symptoms are often dead areas along the veins and margins on leaves.

A few spots on the leaves do little harm to a tree and are far more unsightly than they are injurious. However, leaf spot infections that start early in the growing season can lead to premature defoliation. If it occurs two or more successive years, it can seriously weaken a tree, reduce its growth and increase its susceptibility to bark borers and stem decline diseases.

Chlorosis, a yellowing of leaf blade tissue, is due to a lack of chlorophyll, and may be caused by a number of factors. Probably the most common is iron chlorosis, where iron is unavailable to the plant. In chlorotic leaves, the tissue along the network of veins is green while the interveinal tissue is yellowish green to yellow. If severe, the leaves may be dwarfed, scorched along the leaf margin, or brown spotted between the veins. Trees under severe stress become stunted, have dead terminal branches, and may die. Yellowing of leaves may also be caused by compacted soils, root damage, and other nutrient deficiencies.

Leaf scorch is a widespread, non-infectious disorder that can occur on any species of tree or shrub. In mild cases of scorch, the leaves remain attached and little damage results. In severe cases the leaves may drop prematurely. Scorch usually develops on broad-leaved plants as irregular yellowing, browning or bronzing of tissues along the leaf margin and between the veins. Scorch on leaves is due to an insufficient supply of water. Any of a great number of mechanical or physiological conditions that reduce sap flow in the roots, trunks, branches, stems or twigs can result in scorch. Determining the specific cause or combination of causes for scorch is a diagnostic challenge.

Leaf diseases caused by pathogens are diagnosed by identifying the specific causal agent. These usually produce fruiting bodies (often black or brown pinhead size pustules) on the necrotic tissue of the leaf. Often only one or two pathogens occur frequently on leaves of specific tree species. The presence of fruiting bodies on typical symptoms is sufficient for a tentative diagnosis of the disease. Often this is accomplished with a hand lens or a dissecting microscope.

A relatively new procedure now available to arborists uses ELISA (*Enzyme Linked Immusorbent Assay*) to detect Phythopthora and bacterial leaf scorch. This new technology permits rapid, on the spot diagnosis, even if the sample has deteriorated or the causal organism is no longer viable.

LEAF DISEASES ON DECIDUOUS CONIFERS

Needles or leaf scales on deciduous conifers often are retained and function on the plant for 2, 3, or more years. Needle loss, therefore, on evergreen is more serious than on deciduous plants and damage to first year needles is more serious than that on second year needles. Lesions on evergreens have fewer descriptive names than for broadleaf trees. They are usually **needle blights**, **needle casts**, or **rusts**. Symptoms of blights and casts are quite similar. The causal fungi cause yellow, brown to red spotting or banding of the needles. As infection progresses, these areas gradually enlarge and merge, with the entire needle dying and turning brown. Some fungi infect needles in the spring, others in the fall. Infections are most often seen on the lower part of the tree. Black or brown *fruiting bodies* of the causal fungus form on the lesions. These can be observed with a hand lens or dissecting microscope. Severe infections over two or more years can result in twig dieback and decline.

LEAF AND TWIG DISEASES

Many diseases that are most readily observed on the twigs actually began as leaf or flower diseases. Twig diseases are usually known as **blights, cankers, galls,** or **witches' brooms**. Most are caused by fungi, but two that are caused by bacteria are fire blight and crown gall.

Blight diseases are usually restricted to current season or one year old wood. Leaves and twigs die back from the twig tip and the persisting brown leaves and dead branch tips make the infected plants unsightly. Droplets of bacterial ooze form on overwintering fire blight cankers and fruiting bodies similar to those found on leaves occur on the twigs of fungal blights.

Although the causal agent for **crown gall** is a bacterium, most **galls** on stems result from the activity of insects. Galls are overgrowth of tissue that initially are white or flesh-colored but become irregular, rough, corky, or woody with age. The outer surface becomes dark brown or black. The gall tissue interferes with the normal transport of water and food supplies in the stem. The amount of plant decline is related to the percentage of stem disrupted or girdled by the gall tissue.

Cankers are the most common, widespread and destructive of the stem diseases. Cankers are localized lesions, usually sunken, in bark of twigs or stems. The lesions usually kill the vascular cambium and may enter sapwood. The dead bark may fall away leaving an open wound. Cankers are most destructive to the plant when entire twigs or stems are girdled, thus killing the distal portion of the plant. Large or multiple cankers may kill the affected tree or shrub. Most canker pathogens enter through wounds. Some invade healthy, vigorously growing tissue but most invade tissue of plants that are environmentally stressed. Fruiting bodies of the causal fungi are found on the dead bark above canker lesions. They can be seen with a hand lens or dissecting microscope. Shaving the bark with a knife or razor blade will make them more conspicuous. Patches of white resin commonly form on the bark in cankered areas of evergreen trees. Canker diseases are rarely fatal on mature trees (chestnut blight being the exception), but they cause amenity trees to rapidly lose their attractive appearance and structural integrity.

Witches' brooms on trees result from the multiple growth of twigs at the terminal portion of a stem. Normal twig extension is disrupted. The brooms are seldom winter hardy and the twig tip dies. Brooms are unattractive and undesirable.

STEM AND ROOT DISEASES

Stem and root diseases are usually rots and declines. **Rots** are a discoloration, disintegration, and ultimate softening of plant tissue resulting from fungal or bacterial infection. Rot usually follows a succession of primary and secondary invaders. Rotting of absorbing roots may occur within weeks, but rotting of large roots and trunks takes years. Rots are more common on succulent plants than on woody plants, but the fungus *Armillaria* attacks hundreds of species of

> *Many diseases that are most readily observed on the twigs actually began as leaf or flower diseases.*

fruit, forest and amenity trees. *Armillaria* "shoestrings" or "fans" appear in decayed areas in the trunk bark, at the root collar, or in the roots. The fungus gradually girdles and kills the tree at the base. The fungus fruiting bodies occur as honey-colored mushrooms that grow from stumps or on the ground near infected roots. Plant death from this disease is greatest during periods of moisture stress or after defoliation.

Decline describes the gradual reduction of growth and vigor of a plant. Decline may proceed for several years. **Dieback** begins with the progressive death of twigs and branches which generally starts at the tips. Decline and dieback may result from injuries, insect defoliation, pathogenic agents, or environmental stress. In many cases, three or more are present. Those factors that most threaten the normal root functions are often involved in declines.

SYSTEMIC DISEASES

Some pathogens are localized in the tree and others are able to invade the entire tree (roots, stems and leaves) within a few weeks or months. The latter result is called a systemic disease. Those systemic pathogens that inhabit the inner bark or outer sapwood often kill the host plant. The ***pathogen*** can be a fungus, MLO, bacterium, or nematode. *Fungi* invade the sapwood and usually cause light to dark streaks to form as a ring or series of brown dots in the current season growth. Infected tissue cannot transport water and nutrients to leaves. Leaves on infected branches wilt, turn dull green to yellow, then brown and usually drop prematurely. Trees in the red oak group infected with *Ceratocystis* die within one growing season; elms infected with *Ceratocystis* die within two growing seasons. Verticillium has a wide host range, invades the host more slowly, and may kill only major branches, but often kills entire trees. The causal fungus can be cultured from infected wood in the laboratory.

Mycoplasma-like organisms (***MLO's***) invade the bark and usually cause a darkening of the inner phloem tissue. Infected tissue cannot transport food materials to the roots. The roots starve and the tree usually appears to die suddenly in the spring after leaf emergence. The causal organism can be identified in infected tissue by microscopic observation. **Bacteria** that invade systemically are usually in the heartwood. Although this wood is beneficial in providing tree stability, it is not essential for growth or reproduction. Bacterial wetwood can occur in many species of trees and cause branch dieback. It primarily disfigures trees when light or dark streaks of liquid seep out of cracks or wounds and flow down the bark. The liquid is toxic and prevents healing of branch pruning cuts. **Nematodes** have recently been recognized as cause of a systemic disease in pines. The nematodes primarily inhabit the resin canals in the wood and the water transport system of the tree becomes clogged. The tree appears to die suddenly, the needles turn off-green to totally brown. Pine wilt disease usually occurs only on trees that have suffered environmental stress. Nematodes can be separated from infected wood and identified in the laboratory.

> *Some pathogens are localized in the tree and others are able to invade the entire tree (roots, stems and leaves) within a few weeks or months.*

INSECTS

When you look closely at any woody plant during the spring or summer, you are likely to find insects or insect relatives. Some of the insects are ***beneficial*** and others can damage the plant. Some attack only specific host plants and others are general feeders. Plant identification and recognition of damage symptoms are important first steps in the diagnostic process.

Various methods have been devised to sample, or estimate, the numbers of insects or mites on trees and shrubs. Sample procedures should

✓ PROBLEMS CHECKLIST

SITING, SELECTING, AND PLANTING PROBLEMS:
- Soil
- Climate
- Site
- Improper Planting

MAINTENANCE PROBLEMS:
- Chemical Misapplication
- Construction Injury
- Animal Damage
- Air pollution
- Mechanical Injury

DISEASE PROBLEMS:

DECIDUOUS TREE LEAF DISEASES
- Leaf spots
- Blight
- Rust
- Anthracnose
- Scorch
- Blotch
- Scab
- Powdery mildew
- Chlorosis

CONIFER LEAF DISEASES
- Blights
- Rusts
- Casts

LEAF AND TWIG DISEASES
- Blight
- Gall
- Canker
- Witches' broom

STEM AND ROOT DISEASES
- Rots
- Decline

SYSTEMIC DISEASES
- Fungi
- Bacteria
- MLOs
- Nematodes

---

1. use a common sampling unit,
2. be consistent with the feeding habits of the pest,
3. use an adequate number of samples,
4. standardize the sampling procedure and
5. keep a written record of date, location and person sampling.

The samples may consist of
1. counting of insects on plant parts,
2. counting the number of insects seen during a 1or 2 minute search,
3. holding a sample tray beneath plant foliage and striking with a short stick,
4. counting of fecal pellets or eggs, or
5. using pheromones to physically trap specific moths or beetles.

When sampling for pests, the monitor should also look for predators, evidence of parasitism, or signs of insect disease.

Insect-caused damage symptoms can be grouped into the following cate-

> *Some insects are beneficial and others can damage the plant.*

> *Insects that suck plant juices from leaves include aphids, leafhoppers, plant bugs, lace bugs, spittlebugs, thrips and armored and soft scales*

gories: sucking insects, leaf chewing insects, mining insects, boring insects, and gall forming insects. Numerous textbooks are available that provide details on insect morphology, life cycle, damage, and control procedures.

SUCKING INSECTS

Insects that suck plant juices from leaves include aphids, leafhoppers, plant bugs, lace bugs, spittlebugs, thrips and armored and soft scales.

Aphids are the most common of the sucking insects. They are soft-bodied, slow moving insects that feed on young, succulent growth. They usually do not seriously injure the plant. The greatest damage may be from the sticky, sugary excrement (honeydew) that falls on automobiles or furniture below infested trees. Aphid colonies have many natural enemies.

Leafhoppers come in a variety of colors. Feeding damage may appear as stippling, browning, or curling and withering of leaves. When disturbed, leafhoppers usually scoot sideways along the underside of leaves.

Lace bugs feed on the underside of leaves on a number of trees and shrubs. The affected leaves appear pale or white stippled, similar to spider mite damage.

Spittlebugs are commonly found on evergreens. Larvae produce a frothy mass of spittle on young twigs. They are unsightly but rarely inflict damage on mature plants.

Thrips are tiny insects that rasp and suck juice from flowers and buds. Leaves may be distorted as they unfold.

Armored scales have a hard, flat crusty scale covering over their soft bodies. They are attached to the young stem. Scales have crawler stages that are susceptible to management.

Soft scales are frequently larger than armored scales. Some move about as adults. They do not secrete a horny covering. A related scale, the cottony maple scale, produces a cottony wax covering. Scales have crawler stages that are susceptible to management.

> *Insects that chew leaves include caterpillars, sawflies, leaf beetles, weevils and scarab beetles.*

CHEWING INSECTS

Insects that chew leaves include caterpillars, sawflies, leaf beetles, weevils and scarab beetles. Some including the bagworm, case bearers, webworms and tent caterpillars are tent- or case-making insects.

Caterpillars are the leaf chewing larvae of butterflies and moths. These worm-like insects come in various sizes, shapes and colors. They may eat the entire leaf, eat holes in leaves, eat only the green tissue between the veins (*skeletonize*) or eat only the upper or lower surface of a leaf (*window-feeding*). Some make shelters for protection from the weather and natural enemies (bagworms live inside cases and carry them about, casebearers construct tubular or cylindrical cases, tent caterpillars build web nests in the crotches of twigs and leave the nest to feed on foliage at night).

Sawflies resemble caterpillars but are the larval stages of wasps. Most are leaf chewers, some are maggot-like leaf miners.

Leaf beetle larvae and adults both feed on plant leaves. Larvae window feed on leaf tissue where only the lower plant tissue is eaten away. Adult beetles feed on the entire leaf.

Weevil feeding damage often appears as a crescent-shaped notch cut out of a leaf edge. Root weevils also feed on plant roots in the soil.

Scarab beetle (May or June beetles) adults feed on foliage at night and sometimes in such numbers that they defoliate small trees.

MINING INSECTS

Miners are insects that feed between the upper and lower surfaces of individual leaves. The insects are difficult to see but the trails they create in the leaves are distinctive. One is a serpentine, winding or S-shaped trail; the other is a blotch-mine which leaves a brown, irregularly shaped pattern on the leaf blade. Mines may be small or encompass most of the leaf. Miners may be serious aesthetically but seldom weaken the tree.

BORING INSECTS

Borers are larval stages of insects that tunnel in the wood of twigs, stems, trunks and roots of trees. **Bark beetles** lay eggs just beneath the bark and the larvae feed in the cambial region in all directions from the egg gallery. Some **Flatheaded** and **round headed borers** feed mainly in the sapwood at first, but then each grub mines deeper into the stem as it becomes larger. Others are phloem-feeders with occasional departures into the sapwood. Food and water translocation in the plant is disrupted and the stem is mechanically weakened. Borers usually attack only trees that have been weakened or injured by other stresses; they seldom successfully attack healthy trees. Close inspection of the trees is essential to confirm borer problems. Borer emergence holes are small, but often distinctive in size and shape.

✓ INSECTS / MITES CHECKLIST

CHEWING INSECTS:
- caterpillars
- casebearers
- sawflies
- tent caterpillars
- weevils
- bagworms
- leaf beetles
- scarab beetles
- webworms

SUCKING INSECTS:
- aphids
- leafhoppers
- armored scales
- soft scales
- lace bugs
- plant bugs
- armored scales
- thrips

MINERS

BORERS:
- bark beetles
- flatheaded wood borers
- clear wing borers
- round headed wood borers

GALLS:
- galls from mites
- galls from wasps
- galls from adelgids
- leaf rollers
- galls from eriophyid mites
- galls from midges
- leaf tiers

MITES

GALL FORMING INSECTS

Galls are abnormal growths that appear as warts or bumps on leaves or twigs. They are of many shapes and sizes but each is characteristic of the insect or mite that causes it. Often a part of the life cycle of the gall-producing animal is spent inside the gall. Galls may be produced by midges, wasps, psyllids, or mites. Galls produced on leaves by insects cause little plant injury but are unsightly. Galls on stems and twigs can cause plant injury and may need to be removed and destroyed.

MITES

Mites are not insects but are a closely related group.

Mites are not insects but are a closely related group. Spider mites suck sap from leaves, and give foliage a whitish, silverish or stippled appearance. Stress factors, especially extended dry weather, promote high mite populations on most deciduous trees, whereas cool weather is beneficial for some conifer mites (cool season mites). Mites are most active on the lower leaf surface. They are small (pin-point size) and difficult to see without a hand lens. Since infestation is greatest in late summer, little permanent injury occurs on otherwise healthy woody plants.

CHAPTER SUMMARY

- Diagnosis is the process of identifying the cause of a specific plant problem; it requires acute observational skills and detailed botanical knowledge.
- Plant problems can be caused by environmental or climatic changes or by living organisms (such as fungi, bacteria, viruses, insects, or mites for example). Diagnosticians use categorization techniques to evaluate observations and facilitate identification of the causal agent.
- The diagnosis tool kit permits examination of roots, stems, and leaves. The job is easier, faster, and more complete when the proper equipment is available.
- Many plant problems are associated with improper siting, selecting, planting, or maintenance.
- PHC recognizes that diseases and insects are frequently specific to the plant and locality.

CHAPTER 9

Technical Resources and Strategies

INTRODUCTION

> *PHC practitioners, during the course of regular operations, need timely information on a broad range of subjects...*

PHC is a significant change in strategy, compared to the traditional methods and solutions of tree care professionals. More than any other approach to landscape management, PHC depends heavily on information collection, delivery of the crucial information to professionals, and use of all current information for informed decision making. PHC demands that practicing arborists have channels for accurate, up-to-date technical information and resources.

PHC practitioners, during the course of regular operations, need timely information on a broad range of subjects, from current disease control recommendations or guidelines on local ordinances governing pesticides, to sources and prices of supplies and materials. Just as the range of subjects that are relevant to PHC is broad, the sources of this vital information cover many bases. These suggested resources include courses and training programs, extension advisors, university researchers and specialists, library searches, key reference texts/manuals, and professional experience (personal, and from other plant care professionals). Interdisciplinary communication networks link commercial practitioners with specialists or consultants in areas like biological controls, environmental resource management, or other information bases relevant to PHC management strategies. This information resource base provides substantial information to support individual PHC programs on a local basis, or on a global scale.

EXTENSION AGENTS/UNIVERSITY RESEARCHERS/SPECIALISTS

Extension advisors are a resource for all geographical site information, local pest ordinances, checklists on key pests and key plants in the area, and much more information pertinent to management of a PHC program. Extension advisors also provide pamphlets, flyers, or lists (at a nominal charge or free of charge) to help local arborists remain current on these subjects. Similar materials can be available from University staff, in particular those individuals involved directly in PHC-related research in programs such as horticulture, plant pathology, entomology, urban forestry, botany, or landscape architecture.

FACILITATED LIBRARY SEARCHES

Many libraries now offer computerized literature searches, which can help an arborist pinpoint critical information found in textbooks, audio/visual tapes, or other published materials. The library search (with the help of the librarian) can further help to find information not available in the immediate area, and usually these materials can be borrowed through an inter-library loan. A Compendium of Information on Plant Health Care, by Dorrance et al., 1993, available on electronic medium, contains a broad, continually updated listing of references relevant to PHC practice. This compendium includes an alphabetized subject index from which keywords can be selected to guide an in-depth library search, when more facts are needed. The compendium and additional key references on specific topics are listed below:

SUGGESTED KEY REFERENCES (LITERATURE) FOR SPECIFIC TOPICS

ON THE OVERALL PHC CONCEPT (ALSO CALLED IPM OR OTHER ACRONYMS):

Dorrance, A.E., R.D. Neely, A.G. Endress, M.A. Smith, G.R. Smith, and J.E. Appleby. 1993. A Compendium of Information on Plant Health Care Including Disease, Insect, Weeds and Cultural Practices. Illinois Natural History Survey. Available on electronic medium through International Society of Arboriculture and National Arborist Association.

Olkowski, W. and H. Olkowski. 1983. Integrated Pest Management for Park Managers. A training manual. John Muir Institute, Inc., National Capital Region, National Park Service.

Nielsen, D.G. 1983. Integrated Pest Management (IPM). Plants and Gardens, Brooklyn Botanic Garden Record 40:70-72.

ON WOODY PLANT IDENTIFICATION:

Dirr, M. 1977. Manual of Woody Landscape Plants. Stipes Publishing Co., Champaign, IL. 536 pp.

ON KEY PLANTS/KEY STRESS:

Raupp, M.J., J. A. Davidson, J. J. Homes, and J. L. Hellman. 1985. "The Concept of Key Plants in Integrated Pest Management for Landscapes." Journal of Arboriculture 11:29-34.

Local extension experts help identify specific problem-prone plants to avoid, and can aid in the selection of better alternative plants. In some cases, bulletins or fact-sheets are available to help identify these problems within a geographic region and suggest alternatives for control.

ON SITE INVENTORY AND IMPORTANCE OF SITE FACTORS TO TREE HEALTH:

Harris, R. 1992. (2nd ed.) Arboriculture: Integrated Management of Landscape Trees, Shrubs, and Vines. Prentice-Hall, Inc., Englewood Cliffs, New Jersey 07632

Manion, P. 1991. Tree Disease Concepts. Prentice-Hall, Inc. Englewood Cliffs, New Jersey 07632

Shigo, A. L. 1991. Modern Arboriculture: A Systems Approach to Trees and Their Associates. Durham, NH: Shigo and Trees, Associates.

ON ESTABLISHING A MAP AND THE VALUE OF INDIVIDUAL LANDSCAPE PLANTS:

Council of Tree & Landscape Appraisers. 1992. Guide for Plant Appraisal. International Society of Arboriculture, P.O. Box GG, Savoy, IL 61874.

Raupp, M.J. and R. Noland. 1984. "Implementing Landscape Plant Management Programs in Institutional and Residential Settings." Journal of Arboriculture 10: June 1984.

INTERNET ELECTRONIC INFORMATION RESOURCE

The International Society of Arboriculture (ISA) provides a "home page" on the Internet (electronic information super highway) for persons interested in obtaining Plant Health Care information to maintain an effective Plant Health Care program. The Plant Health Care page provides a one-stop service with connections (links) to electronic information at universities, extension services, and other institutions throughout the world that provide up-to-date research-based plant health care information. The information and recommendations provided by the links are the responsibility of the institution or organization explicitly providing the information. ISA and the University of Illinois Cooperative States Research, Education, and Extension Service (CSREES), which provides technical support for the page, are in no way responsible or liable for the information provided by the links except those that are specifically indicated as being provided by ISA or the University of Illinois CSREES.

PROFESSIONAL EXPERIENCE

> *Professional experience is one of the most valuable resources for building a record of information pertinent to PHC practices.*

Professional experience is one of the most valuable resources for building a record of information pertinent to PHC practices. The experiences and recommendations of other plant care professionals in the region, as well as personal business experiences and records, can provide invaluable, specific reference information that may not be available in any other form. PHC program supervisors need to establish channels and networks to access the experience-based knowledge and advice of others in the profession, in order to conduct accurate programs and make sound management decisions. The professional organizations of practicing arborists [e.g. the International Society of Arboriculture (ISA), the National Arborist Association (NAA), the Associated Landscape Contractors of America (ALCA), National Landscape Association (NLA) and others] are excellent forums for exchange of this crucial and necessary information. PHC arborists should have passed the *Certified Arborist* examination offered by ISA.

The business time and materials records of the individual arborist provide real documentation on exactly which species repeatedly required management action and demanded the most resources for treatment and maintenance.

Consultants or specialists in disciplines relevant to the PHC program are additional resources (much like anesthesiologists or cardiologists might serve as resources for a general medical practitioner). These include biological control research/production laboratories, which may have the facilities and resources to handle scientific and regulatory tasks which are not feasible for an individual PHC practitioner. In-depth research on environmental impacts of some PHC programs might be assessed via appropriate specialists. The communications networks ideally should include on-line computer-based delivery systems for rapid, wide-range dispersal of the information, and opportunity for feedback from the practitioners using this information.

The above is by no means a comprehensive list of resources available for PHC, but instead provides some suggestions for building a reference file. A Compendium of Information on Plant Health Care in particular, is the result of a recent effort to provide an integrated, computerized data base on PHC materials, and an improved information transfer system. This reference was compiled from a wide range of IPM-related resources nationwide, has been indexed to facilitate computer-aided searches, and has been formatted to allow continual updating. As new information becomes available, this compendium will be regularly updated for use by PHC practitioners.

PHC STRATEGIES

PHC emphasizes an environmentally-sensitive spectrum of techniques for landscape maintenance and protection. Multiple strategies for prevention, avoidance, and treatment, borrowed from several different disciplines and integrating diverse methodologies, are directed toward the common goal of managing tree health-related problems in the landscape. A well-orchestrated system of interlocking tactics are aimed to constrain, rather than eliminate, landscape pests and problems. This overall approach not only creates a powerful, effective means of long-term management, but tends to minimize reliance on chemical applications for pests which have already become damaging.

Treatment of existing problems, which has historically been the arborists' most common management strategy, can now be regarded as a "last resort" tactic, taken in the event that prevention or avoidance fails to circumvent a disease or insect problem. Chemical applications are avoided in favor of alternatives due to increasing governmental pressures, changing restrictions against use of some relied-on products, and concerns over residues in ground water, or chemical effects on people in or near treatment areas. Treatment options have shifted away from eliminating pests with broad applications of chemical pesticides to multi-dimensional, ecologically-sound strategies. These strategies to reduce pest populations to nondamaging levels are not disruptive to natural controls and combine chemical, biological, and cultural/mechanical management.

The following section provides an organized, detailed breakdown of the management strategies available within the Plant Health Care approach, with definitive emphasis on strategies which preclude the development of pest outbreaks, or of problems that require treatment intervention. A synopsis of treatment options, including chemical, biological, and cultural controls, are discussed. This section is not intended as a "step by step" set of directives. Each landscape situation under the management of a PHC practitioner may require a unique approach to maximize the results. Rather, this section outlines the options available, and gives examples of how diverse management measures can be used together to obtain the best possible results.

> *Treatment options have shifted away from broad applications of chemical pesticides...*

MANAGEMENT STRATEGIES

PREVENTION/AVOIDANCE

With PHC, the focus of all management strategies shifts away from the pest or problem and shifts to the landscape plants, with the goal of increasing and sustaining tree vigor by reducing stress. Strategies for prevention or avoidance of landscape pest problems are another cornerstone of the PHC approach. These include long-range solutions like selection of superior plant species or cultivars, site modifications, or cultural practices, which encourage the vigor of the plant and minimize susceptibility to pests. Management strategies that completely preclude the need for treatment intervention are the most satisfying for both the plant care professional and the client, and most cost-effective.

Plant Selection. Arborists are usually called in for maintenance of landscapes that have previously been installed, but frequently, PHC practitioners have the opportunity to make recommendations for plant selection in the landscape. Initial selection of landscape plants that are naturally resistant to pests is an excellent, highly effective strategy. Certain groups of landscape trees and shrubs tend to remain relatively free of problems, whereas other common species are highly susceptible to recurrent attacks. The latter group of plants are also commonly found on the "key plant/key stress" lists described earlier in Chapter 7. Superior plant selections will not only include species with resistance to common pests, but also the most site and climate tolerant species. Each site has inherent environmental conditions that will guide decisions on which plants can best survive; each tree species differs in its own requirements for these factors. Plants which are tolerant of adverse conditions, such as a prolonged drought or poor soils, will not be predisposed to pest attack like more sensitive selections. Simple avoidance of problem-prone species in favor of more tolerant plants is a way to avoid the need for management strategies or treatment steps during subsequent maintenance of the site.

Certain tree species (red maple, for example) have some natural genetic capacity to adapt to a variety of site conditions (they are able to acclimate and survive when conditions become unfavorable, whereas other species simply decline). This is a valued characteristic, but still, proper selection of tree to the site (and maintenance of ideal site conditions) will afford more assurance of success in plant and site compatibility. Trees should be matched to sites that offer:

- adequate area for root expansion (and excellent planting soil),
- sufficient area for canopy growth and expansion (without distortion of the tree's natural mature habit),
- adequate moisture and drainage.

Trees with shallow root systems should not be selected for sites near pavement or traffic, as this will invite later root zone stress and attending problems with tree stress and decline. Trees with broad spreading mature canopies should be avoided in favor of upright growth forms for planting spaces adjacent to buildings. The hardiness zone of the site must be matched to the hardiness of the tree — it's ability to survive low temperatures. Similar considerations regarding light levels, high temperatures, and other factors govern selection of ideal trees for a planting site — trees that are most likely to thrive at the site, and not be susceptible to pest attack.

Placement or Design. Closely related to selection for superior plants is careful design of landscapes which build in management measures. Monoculture plantings (with repetitive placement of the same species, or worse, the same cultivar on a single site) are discouraged, since this type of design makes

> *Plants which are tolerant of adverse conditions, such as a prolonged drought or poor soils, will not be predisposed to pest attack like more sensitive selections.*

> *Diversification of species will inhibit the spread of any single, specialized plant pathogen or insect...*

it easy for a successful pest species to travel quickly through a site causing serious damage. Instead, landscape designs should blend together a diverse range of tree and shrub species. Diversification of species will inhibit the spread of any single, specialized plant pathogen or insect, and minimize losses on a client's property in the event that a pest invades the site. Diversification within a landscape mimics the mix of plants in nature, and therefore further enforces natural controls. When the same or similar, related species are repeated in a landscape design, the plants should ideally be located with separating distances to minimize pest spread.

Landscape plants that are massed in planting beds are more protected from severe environmental stresses than trees or shrubs planted singly. This protective design measure can take advantage of larger, deeper prepared soil areas with common mulch for grouped plants, which minimizes, for example, low temperature injuries or wind damage in the winter. Protective screens, provided either by dense plantings or structural materials, can provide similar protection from climatic extremes for other sensitive plants in the landscape. Plants which are normally understory (protected) plants in nature (for example, azaleas) are likely to suffer greater damage from pest infestations when planted openly in the sun and wind, due to the additional stress imposed by exposure. Design of protective taller plants in mass with the sensitive species, or installation of fencing or lath which fulfills the same function, will provide similar control. In all cases, plants must be installed in planting sites which will provide adequate resources for continued long term growth and development, without the need for unusual maintenance intervention (e.g. hedge-style pruning or root pruning) to keep the plant within the bounds of the site.

Cultural Practices. The cultural management measures discussed in this section are considered preventive steps, since they are designed to invigorate landscape plants and make them less susceptible to future attack by pests (avoid predisposition of plants to pests). Many of these same cultural management measures which are employed as preventive measures to pest attack will be repeated below as cultural treatment techniques, used in the management of observed pest problems in the next section.

> *Cultural management measures are considered preventive steps, since they are designed to invigorate landscape plants and make them less susceptible to future attack by pests.*

A series of simple, effective cultural practices can be used to modify the landscape habitat, making it less attractive for pests (by removing places where pests overwinter or breed) and more favorable for the natural predators of the pest. For example, some damaging plant pathogens, notably, the rust diseases, require two hosts to complete a life cycle. One host might be the ornamental landscape plant of interest to the PHC practitioner, and the alternate host might be a wild or native plant in the vicinity. When the alternate hosts are removed from the site and (when possible) the surrounding area, the life cycle of the pest is broken, and the disease can be effectively curbed.

Other pests might require debris piles, weeds, or infested plant material to overwinter. Cultural practices that enforce sanitation in the landscape essentially remove these sources of inoculum, and prevent reinfestation of a landscape by new outbreaks of the same pests the subsequent season. Sanitation also includes preventive inspection of any new plants or seeds brought into the landscape, to avoid introducing pests cultivated at a garden center or landscape nursery.

Proper pruning technique, in particular, is a critical part of a preventive strategy for landscape plants maintenance. When limbs are removed from a tree, either to open up a canopy, eliminate a dangerous obstruction with a roof line or power lines, or to remove parasitic, unproductive tissues from a tree canopy interior, the pruning must be conducted according to the well-estab-

> *Proper pruning technique is a critical part of a preventive strategy for landscape plants maintenance.*

lished guidelines. The 3-step pruning technique allows removal of limbs without further damage to the tree, and leaves a clean, well-shaped cutting wound.

Improper pruning techniques, on the other hand, may result in stripped bark or large, unsightly wounds and tree stubs that are difficult for the tree to repair naturally. This may further stress the plant, encouraging attack by other pests. In this case, poor, unprofessional tree maintenance practices can actually shorten the life and impair the health of a plant. Similarly, pruning for shrubs and hedges requires specific, professionally-guided techniques to maintain plant vigor and discourage attack by other organisms. Shrubs that are pruned according to the natural growth habit of the plant (with selective, careful removal of old, dead, diseased canes and minimal change in plant habit or structure) will be able to combat disease or insect attack with renewed vigor. In contrast, shrubs that are severely sheared into geometrical shapes, or cut back without regard for natural growth form, will suffer stress from imbalanced root and shoot systems and be unable to repair severe pruning wounds. In this latter case, the shrubs are particularly susceptible to environmental stress or pest attack, which will further weaken the plant. In some cases, a move away from these severe, damaging pruning practices in favor of more natural, invigorating techniques will require some convincing consultation and redirection of client preferences. Again, specific directives on pruning techniques to maintain healthy, vigorous trees and shrubs and maximize natural protective defenses against pests are provided in references earlier in this chapter and in the Compendium.

Numerous other cultural tactics for site preparation, which vary according to the specifics of the landscape site, can be employed to help avoid or protect against future stress problems. Application of protective mulch around planting beds, for example, discourages weed infestation and provides a temperature buffer. Site modifications to improve drainage for plants are effective as they alleviate a stress condition (overly wet planting beds) which could encourage the spread of root rot diseases. In addition, this same cultural management tactic (provision of adequate drainage) will eliminate habitats in the landscape that favor pest breeding and spread.

Other horticultural management practices such as cultivation of the soil (to curb, for example, weed populations), and careful pruning to remove old, weak, or infected branches of plants (to reduce havens for pests) modify the site in favor of plants. Use of proper horticultural transplanting techniques (specific directives available in the Compendium) ensure that landscape plants have adequate and well-aerated root zones, and are able to become stably established on a new site. On the other hand, unprofessional planting tactics (which may restrict a root system, provide inadequate root area or drainage, or stress a plant by transplanting out of season) are likely to predispose a plant to attack by pests which, under non-stressful conditions, would not normally cause damage.

Logical practices which invigorate the landscape plants, such as timely watering and fertilizing, are effective techniques in the same strategy. Slow-release nitrogen fertilizers are of particular value to PHC programs. When applied, they gradually and over a long period provide small quantities to encourage and maintain plant vigor, without excess contamination of groundwater.

MANAGEMENT

Threshold determinations. Management becomes necessary when a pest or other stress problem has exceeded or has the potential to exceed a threshold

> *Management becomes necessary when a pest or other stress problem has exceeded or has the potential to exceed a threshold level...*

level, as described in Chapter 7. Below the threshold, pest populations can usually be tolerated because they do not threaten the health of the landscape plant or mar their aesthetic qualities. Woody plants can cope with substantial insect or pathogen activity before aesthetic value is harmed or before the plant becomes weakened and susceptible to opportunistic secondary pests. But at levels at or above the threshold, treatment intervention is required to maintain plants in top condition. A vigorous plant will tolerate a higher level of pest activity than a declining plant, or than a plant simultaneously combatting drought or other environmental stress. Intervention is required before aesthetic damage or physiological stress (weakening of plant vigor) occurs. Some host-pest combinations have very low thresholds before significant injury occurs, other host-plant combinations do not cause serious damage until the pest populations become very high. For example, even small populations of spruce aphid can cause feeding damage sufficient to significantly weaken and aesthetically destroy a specimen spruce tree. Much higher populations of other aphids can be tolerated by certain shade tree specimens without affecting long-term damage. When management is necessary, elimination of the pest is not the goal. The goal is to maintain or reduce the pest problem to tolerable (acceptable) levels.

There are no specific economic or aesthetic thresholds to cover the majority of landscape pest problems. In agriculture we can calculate yields and economic returns and correlate them to pest damage to develop specific economic thresholds. It is much more difficult to correlate pest damage with the aesthetic returns of the large variety of landscape plants. Threshold levels for landscape plants vary from client to client, from plant to plant, and from pest to pest. Knowledge about the pest and its impact on the plant and the client's perception are necessary to provide a general idea of what the threshold might be.

Timing. Whereas preventative/avoidance measures will be conducted in the absence of any pest problem, treatment control measures are in response to pest observation (above or approaching predetermined threshold levels). Identifying when a pest will become a problem or when it is a problem is the first step in correctly timing management strategies. Management should be initiated before the problem causes significant damage. Monitoring is necessary to determine when the pests will reach this threshold. The time between when management is taken and when the response to management occurs needs to be taken into account when determining thresholds. Damage may exceed acceptable levels between the period of time from treatment to response.

> *Whereas preventative/avoidance control measures will be conducted in the absence of any pest problem, management measures are in response to pest observation.*

Determining the point at which intervention is necessary requires regular, thorough monitoring. It also requires technical knowledge on seasonal patterns of pest development, population dynamics, pest life cycles, and information on all treatment options (as emphasized later in this chapter). Armed with this information, the PHC practitioner will design appropriate treatment measures and may consult with scientists and specialists. When chemical treatments are warranted, PHC gives priority to options that are highly specific, timed and localized (spot treatments), rather than to broad-spectrum, indiscriminate cover sprays.

Tools are available that will help with the timing of management. Degree Day forecasting, based on temperature accumulations, and plant phenological events can be used to predict pest development. These tools assist in timing management activities to coincide with susceptible stages in insect pests' lifecycles. They are tools that can help predict when insect events should be happening, but do not indicate whether pests are present. They do not replace

> *Timing of pesticide application should be before threshold injury levels occur and must coincide with a susceptible status of the pest organism.*

active monitoring. Pheromone traps (described below) can be used to monitor insect presence, activity (stages in the lifecycle) and populations.

Timing of pesticide application should be before threshold injury levels occur, but also must coincide with a susceptible status of the pest organism. Treatment applications that are applied too early (for example, on a yearly schedule that may not consider variations in actual pest life cycle and activity) are a waste of time and materials. In these cases, it is possible that the pest problem would never have reached serious proportions and treatment could have been avoided altogether. Cultural tactics, such as watering to invigorate a drought-stricken plant, may have been sufficient to prevent a damaging build-up of the pest.

On the other hand, treatments applied too late (after significant, unacceptable injury has occurred) are also wasteful. In these cases, the client will not be satisfied with the outcome of treatment (damaged plants). Pests may have passed beyond a vulnerable stage in their life cycle. For example, a larval stage may be sensitive to chemical spray, whereas the beetle stage in less vulnerable. An actively feeding caterpillar stage will ingest applied pesticides or microbial insecticides such as the stomach poison *Bacillus thuringiensis Kurstaki*, whereas the moth stage of the same insect will not be affected. Synthetic chemical pesticide treatments applied too late can actually worsen the pest problem. They may disturb a natural ecosystem just at the time when a pests' predators or parasites have already caused a decline in the pest population. Timing is not only critical for synthetic pesticides, but also relevant to microbial/biological treatments and other management tactics. Many biologically derived products and natural enemies (parasites & predators) are effective only against certain life stages of pests. Timing of fertilizer applications (for example, to help invigorate a weakened tree) should coincide with periods of active root growth and water availability.

Localization of treatment. Localized treatments (as opposed to blanket, indiscriminate cover sprays) are a further goal for PHC treatment applications. Spot treatment minimizes side-effects on other organisms or people in a vicinity, and is most efficient in terms of materials use. Localized spot treatments reduce the applicator work time required, and reduce the potential for chemical (or other) build up on a site. PHC practitioners recognize that some trees (even trees of the same species) are more prone to pest attack than others; neighboring trees may not require treatment just because other trees exhibit damage. Localization of a chemical application on a plant (rather than overall coverage) may offer superior management. For example, an infestation of aphids may not be equally distributed throughout the plant. Let's say you are only finding them on the new foliage on the north side of the tree. By concentrating treatments to the area where the aphids are, instead of an overall canopy spray of the tree, you spare some of the natural predators that are feeding on the aphids. The remaining aphids and other pests, you miss with any style of treatment, may still be naturally regulated by the natural enemies that you spared.

> *Determination of a threshold injury level, and careful timing of treatments are precursors to effective treatment under any circumstances.*

To recap, determination of a threshold injury level, and careful timing of treatments are precursors to effective treatment under any circumstances. The use of carefully placed spot treatments is much preferable to blanket cover sprays, in particular for synthetic chemicals (as described below), but in general for all treatments, to conserve materials and time. Each of these prerequisite decisions are possible only given information accumulated during the monitoring process.

MANAGEMENT OPTIONS

> *Cultural management treatments refer to practices which change the physical environment of the site to favor the landscape plants, and discourage survival of pest organisms.*

CULTURAL

Cultural management treatments refer to practices which change the physical environment of the site to favor the landscape plants, and discourage survival of pest organisms. As noted above, many of the same cultural manipulations used as preventative measures are also effective treatments when the pest species is present on site.

Cultural invigoration techniques used to combat observed pest problems include basics like use of good pruning techniques to eliminate dead, stressed, or diseased wood, and careful care of wounds to ensure that attractive ports for pest re-entry are not left on a pruned shrub. Example: aphid infestation is favored when trees have very dense canopies with little aeration (in particular, canopies with dense, and succulent, sucker growth). Careful selective pruning to thin out the canopy and introduce aeration to the interior of the canopy will diminish the rapid population build up of the aphids. This cultural treatment might be used in tandem with an insecticide, to provide more thorough and lasting benefits. Fertilization and watering practices are timed carefully as part of the strategy for eliminating pests and reducing future infestations. Example: In the case of the bronze birch borer, timely watering to invigorate susceptible birch trees can be an exceptionally effective tactic to invigorate a weakened tree and help it combat the pest even after the tree has been attacked.

Sanitation as cultural management includes physical (mechanical and hand) removal of pest infested or diseased plant parts (including measures to collect and burn or destroy inoculum), or manual removal of weeds. Manual removal is not an economically-feasible option for most pests of landscape plants, which tend to occur in great numbers and are very small. However, for fall webworms or tent caterpillars on selected host trees, manual removal (by hand or using pole pruners) can effectively and rapidly eliminate the infestation. Piles of fall leaves or other garden debris may also harbor landscape plant insects over winter, and should therefore be cleared away from the landscape site. These cultural steps to expose pests to winter stress can eliminate or reduce populations. As an example, sanitation around tree bases affords management for birch leaf miner.

> *Sanitation as cultural management includes physical (mechanical and hand removal of pest infested or diseased plant parts or manual removal of weeds.*

When a tree or shrub planting must be removed due to pest damage, the replanting should feature different species of plants. This is a logical treatment, similar to crop rotation for agronomic crops, since it will avoid infestation of new plantings with residual inoculum around the planting site. The concept of crop rotation is quite relevant especially for urban woody plants. Even typically long-lived tree species have drastically shortened life expectancies under the stress of the urban environment. Trees can be categorized into short, medium, and long rotation species, with differing life expectancies in unfavorable urban sites, and representatives from these categories should be mixed and rotated as new replantings are required.

BIOLOGICAL

Biological alternatives to pesticides exist on several levels: multicellular organisms (parasites, predators, natural enemies of pests, allelopathy), microbial organisms (microorganisms or toxins synthesized by microbes), various natural products that manage or monitor pest activity (pheromones, insect growth regulators, traps or baits using natural attractants), and biological management (use of cover crops, or natural/living mulches to manage pests or enhance populations of natural antagonists of the pest).

One beneficial side-effect of reduced pesticide application in a landscape is that natural **biological controls** (predators, pathogens, and parasites of the pest species that already occur on the site) will simultaneously be conserved. In fact, a low level of the landscape pest is required (and must be accepted) in order to maintain biological controls. To maximize the natural biological controls available, any chemical treatment (as noted above) will be introduced only if required to prevent injury above a threshold level, and only as species-specific spot treatments, rigorously timed and targeted to minimize impact on non-target organisms living on site.

Biological control measures include tactics which conserve or enhance the natural populations of parasites, predators, or pathogens that combat pests of landscape plants. Examples include parasitic insects (with larvae that develop inside a pest's body), predators like ladybird beetles and lacewings (which feed on pest insects), and pathogenic diseases (bacteria, fungi or viral organisms) which destroy the pest organism. In fact, because of the presence of these natural biological controls, total eradication of any landscape pest is never the goal of PHC. If the ecosystem were completely devoid of the pest, natural balance would be disrupted, and predators or parasites would die out. This situation would lead to rapid, damaging build up of the pest population if it were ever reintroduced.

To conserve biological controls, chemical spot treatments are timed so as to have minimal detrimental effect on these beneficial organisms. Selective pesticides are given priority, so as not to disturb non-targeted organisms. Selected trees on a property may be excluded from pesticide spraying in order to protect the biological control organisms within. To enhance natural populations, whenever possible, the environment is modified to favor biological controls. Examples include the deliberate incorporation of certain flowers into a landscape site, as nectar and pollen sources to feed populations of parasitic wasps. Populations can be artificially increased by deliberately introducing these organisms into the landscape site. Natural populations could be augmented, or biological controls that are not established on the site could be introduced from an outside source. Most often this measure will be effective against introduced pests (with few or no native controls).

There is a well-established lag that occurs in predator-prey interactions which can make accurate predictions on timing very difficult. Insufficient background data on these biological relationships has been collected to completely avoid timing errors, but in-house and on-the-job research and experience within a particular PHC operation will continuously elucidate these relationships and fine-tune the practitioner's ability to use these controls in subsequent cases.

Artificial introduction of biological controls is a highly specialized management measure which must guarantee that the introduced organism is specifically attracted to the landscape pest (and will not itself become a pest problem). In particular, when natural enemies of damaging landscape pests are deliberately introduced as biological controls, the aid of specialists will be required. Biological control laboratories have the resources to match exotic pests with natural enemies, secure required permits, and recommend steps to ensure successful importation and colonization of a new site. Commercial insectaries now produce and ship beneficial predatory insects for biological control programs, which include green lacewings, ladybird beetles, predatory mites, and Trichogramma wasps (which parasitize moth eggs). Researchers are currently in the process of evaluating other biological controls such as other species of nematodes (for grub control), other bacterial or fungal controls for

> *One beneficial side-effect of reduced pesticide application is that natural biological controls will simultaneously be conserved.*

> *To conserve biological controls, chemical spot treatments are timed so as to have minimal detrimental effect on beneficial organisms.*

pest organisms, and diseases and insects that control weed populations.

Microbial products include the well-known and widely-accepted *Bacillus thuringiensis* (Bt), which has strains that are lethal to specific insects; the related *B. popillae* (milky spore disease) is pathogenic to Japanese beetle grubs. Bt, in particular, is used widely and is marketed in numerous different formulations and application rates. For example, the product "Foray" (Novo Laboratories) is Bt var. Kurstaki which controls gypsy moth, tent caterpillar, and other caterpillar pests. "M-One" is an alternative Bt strain which is effective against larvae (including elm leaf beetle larvae). Other products include virus preparations, such as the gypsy moth nucleopolyhedrosis virus (NPV). NPV has been demonstrated as having minimal effect on other organisms besides the pest gypsy moth. As an example of a biological control using nematodes, "BioSafe" (Biosys) uses *Steinernema carposapsae* to manage pests that typically spend a significant percentage of their life cycles underground. Nematode inoculations have proven effective for containerized soils, and have been used against pests such as some stem boring insects, root weevils, soil-harbored beetle larvae, and chrysanthemum leafminer. These and similar products are marketed and often formulated like synthetic pesticides.

Some of the natural chemical compounds cited above are actually biological derived management, since they are extracted from natural organisms or synthesized to mimic natural compounds, but are not actually the natural organism. These include chemicals which disrupt the pest life cycle, such as insect growth regulators, or pheromones

Traps are commonly-accepted devices for control of pests of humans (e.g., houseflies, mosquitoes, or roaches), and can similarly be introduced to combat whiteflies and other landscape plant pests. Traps can help to detect the presence of pests, determine the stage in the pest life cycle, and give population estimates that guide timing of treatment. Baited traps use specific attractants (for example, synthetic insect pheromones or chemicals produced by plants, or attractant colors like yellow) to entice the insect onto a sticky surface or into an enclosure. They contribute to management strategy since they can identify the ideal time for targeted pesticide application, and avoid wasted, blind applications. For example, a high level of lilac or rhododendron borer moths captured in a trap would alert a PHC practitioner to apply residual insecticides to the landscape plants' bark, since these insect pests will deposit eggs soon after the flying period. The precisely-timed insecticide application will be in effect at the time the newly hatched borers attempt to enter the bark of the plants. Traps can similarly monitor the activity and populations of beneficial insects (potential biological controls) and govern decisions on whether or not further management action is required. Information gained from the trapping of beneficial insects can also prevent ill-timed pesticide applications from eliminating biological controls already in force.

Finally, use of biological management practices include living mulches or natural mulches which suppress pest activity. Trap crops or cover crops (used in similar management programs for agronomic crops) have potential value for some extended landscape or commercial situations as well. Landscapes can deliberately incorporate nectar or food sources or preferred shelters to enhance the establishment of the beneficial organisms cited earlier.

The deliberate use of natural biological controls is an effective and environmentally-conscious technique. Unfortunately, the introduction or encouragement of pathogens or parasites on a site may seem contrary to the practices expected by the client. Biological management measures, perhaps more than any other weapon in the PHC arsenal, may require exceptional attention to consumer education in order to gain acceptance.

> *The deliberate use of natural biological controls is an effective and environmentally-conscious technique*

CHEMICAL

Chemical controls include synthetic pesticides, natural products such as horticultural oils and soaps used to suppress pests, and other natural chemicals like pheromones, growth regulators, juvenile hormones, sterilants, or contraceptives.

Synthetic Chemicals. The well known synthetic pesticides (herbicides, insecticides, fungicides, and related chemicals) include ***contact chemicals***, ***systemic chemicals***, ***stomach poisons***, and ***fumigants***. Synthetic organic pesticides can be categorized as ***chlorinated hydrocarbons***, ***organophosphates***, ***carbamates***, ***pyrethroids***, and ***growth regulators***, but specific formulations and names are too quickly modified and outdated to warrant listing of available products. ***Traps*** or ***baits*** incorporate some of these products.

Public dismay over excessive use of pesticides, potential for toxic damage to applicators and bystanders in a treated area, and overwhelming costs, energy concerns, and legal liabilities associated with dependence on chemical controls, are a large part of the impetus behind the movement toward alternative PHC approaches for landscape maintenance. Survey results have repeatedly shown that property owners are readily willing to use pesticides in their own yards, but prefer targeted rather than blanket sprays. Several states have well-publicized regulations that aim to minimize public exposure to pesticides used in landscape care. Synthetic chemicals are one of the treatment options available to the PHC practitioner. Synthetic chemicals must be used wisely to protect other (beneficial) organisms and to not disrupt the ecosystem.

Chemical pesticides are of most use when used in concert with other PHC techniques. The selective use of herbicides (rather than manual cultivation) to remove weeds around landscape plants, for example, has the advantage that soil is not mechanically disturbed. This reduces the potential for soil erosion and loss. When combined with thorough mulching in a massed planting bed, herbicides can help maintain an attractive, well-groomed landscape appearance.

Materials selection is based on specificity (to the target organism) as well as safety to the applicator. In order to minimize exposure hazards, products with high ***LD50*** numbers are preferred. LD50 refers to the rating of acute toxicity of a material (the lethal dose per kilogram body weight required to kill 50% of laboratory test animals). Materials which fail to break down in the environment after use are avoided by PHC practitioners whenever possible, in order to minimize environmental impact.

Conventional synthetic pesticides are a valuable tool in a PHC program, when used as spot treatments rather than in broad cover sprays, and in combination with other non-chemical techniques. Selective applications and improved methods of application (for example, combination with soaps and oils) allow significant reductions in the amounts of chemical applied. Dosages and application frequencies should be as low as possible, in order to avoid possible build up of resistance in a pest species.

To recap, pesticides as one treatment tactic in a PHC program should be applied:

- as an adjunct or in combination with other tactics as part of a long-term strategy
- when unacceptable injury levels will occur without application
- as spot treatments
- when timed to coincide with susceptible pest stages and activity
- when targeted to be pest-specific with low impact on other organisms
- in low dosages
- when the material has demonstrated limited persistence
- when the material is non-toxic to the applicator or other bystanders

> *Chemical pesticides are of most use when used in concert with other PHC techniques.*

Horticultural Soaps and Oils. Horticultural oil for foliar insects serves to smother or suppress pests, as in the case of scale insects. Early spring or late fall applications of 2% oil will control pests that overwinter on the plant host before damage can begin during the growing season. Other refined formulations have been marketed specifically for use during the growing season. Phytotoxicity coincident with use of horticultural oils has been observed, but is rare, and usually occurs with specimens that are otherwise stressed or unhealthy.

Soaps alone control most soft-bodied insects and mites, but don't offer residual control. Registered synthetic chemical sprays can be used at significantly reduced rates (one half to one tenth the normal recommended concentrations) when soaps, horticultural oils, or other oil formulations are combined in the mixture, and offer enhanced control. Better residual control, enhanced effectiveness against difficult-to-control pests, and effectiveness against a wide range of pests are further advantages of insecticidal soaps. Both laboratory and field tests provide strong justification for combining petrochemical pesticides and soaps, since reduced rates of pesticide provide better control than standard rates alone.

Natural Chemicals. Pheromones refer to natural attractant or repellent compounds. They can be used to confuse an insect into disrupting its natural life cycle behavior, but more typically, pheromones are useful aids to accurate pest monitoring. Attractant pheromones (which are associated with sex or aggregation habits of insects) can be incorporated into sticky traps which then permit the PHC practitioner to very efficiently monitor pest activity and numbers. *Pheromone traps* can guide the professional in gauging how quickly a pest population has developed, and deciding on the most appropriate timing for treatment applications based on these population estimates.

Attractant pheromones that have been identified and used to monitor pest activity include compounds specific for several boring insects, bark beetles, and moths (see specific updates on pheromone identification and availability in the Compendium). Pheromones, allomones, and kairomones include feeding attractants, sex attractants, and repellents produced by insects (or synthesized to match products produced by insects) that can be used to disrupt or monitor pest life cycles.

Other potential natural chemical treatments include use of insect growth regulators like juvenile hormones that arrest pest development (prevent sexual maturity), sterilants, or contraceptives to reduce breeding. Botanical compounds (toxins) derived from plants, such as ryania and pyrethrum, are other natural alternatives to synthetic chemicals. Pyrethrin-based compounds called Pyrethroids (for example, "Tempo" marketed by Mobay) allow low application rates and effective insect management. These natural botanical compounds, however, are not necessarily safer or less toxic than synthetics, simply by virtue of being organically derived. Although chemical in nature, some of these tactics may be considered under biological management measures as well.

COMBINED TACTICS

Plant Health Care management strategies depend on a mix of two or more tactics, together or in sequence, to obtain more thorough, long-lasting results than any single method alone. Table 9-1 provides a list of the variety of tactics available, from which the most effective strategies can be assembled. For example, baited pheromone traps (natural chemical management) can be used to pre-

TABLE 9–1. PHC Management Strategies and Tactics

PREVENTION/AVOIDANCE (STEPS TAKEN BEFORE PESTS ARE OBSERVED)

Plant Selection
- Resistance
- Site/climate tolerance

Plant Placement or Design
- Avoidance of monocultures
- Diversification
- Separating distances
- Massed or grouped plantings
- Protective screens

Cultural Practices
- Eliminate alternate hosts
- Sanitation/removal of debris
- Proper pruning technique
- Site preparation
  — Protective mulch
  — Redirected/improved drainage
- Horticultural management
  — Soil cultivation/weed elimination
  — Proper transplanting technique
  — Plant invigoration techniques
    - Timely watering
    - Fertilization

TREATMENT OPTIONS (STEPS TAKEN TO COMBAT OBSERVED PESTS)

Cultural
- Horticultural management
  — Fertilization, watering, cultivation
  — Pruning and removal
  — Wound care
- Sanitation
- Manual pest removal
- Crop rotation

Biological
- Multicellular organisms
  — Conserve or enhance populations of predators, parasites, or pathogens of pests
  — Artificially increase populations of predators, parasites, or pathogens of pests
  — Microbial organisms and products
    - Other natural products
    - Juvenile hormones, pheromones
    - Traps and baits
- Biological management
  — Natural/living mulches, trap, protective, or cover crops to enhance natural enemies or control pests

Chemical
- Horticultural soaps and oils
- Natural chemical controls
  — Pheromones, allomones, kairomones
  — Juvenile hormones
  — Sterilants, contraceptives
  — Botanical toxins
- Synthetic chemical pesticides.

Combined tactics
- In most cases, a management strategy that combines tactics from different categories provides maximum results.

> *Plant Health Care management strategies depend on a mix of two or more tactics, in tandem or in sequence, to obtain more thorough, long-lasting results than any single method alone.*

dict insect life cycle behavior, and determine ideal timing for synthetic chemical sprays for the pest. As another example of the interrelationship between organisms in the landscape, aphid management will simultaneously eliminate the honeydew symptom that irritates property owners and attracts other pests like flies or ants. Environmental protection is emphasized (only targeted, well-timed spray treatments are used), and the effectiveness of the chemical spray treatment is heightened through guidance of natural chemical monitoring. PHC programs need to be organized to maximize communication and interaction between professional specialists in certain related areas (e.g., biological control laboratories) and field personnel who will select from among treatment options. Pest management strategies will be strengthened when all information on current research and new approaches is consistently available to everyone involved in the process of landscape protection.

Overall development of management strategies may integrate many of the compatible tactics outlined above, and multiple approaches and combinations to the same landscape maintenance/management challenge may be available for consideration (e.g., alternative sets of tactics that may achieve the same results). It is important to realize that while management tactics are varied and require significant background knowledge, the PHC approach *should not* be regarded as a strategy that is "too complex" to implement. Decisions on specific management strategies are guided by evaluations — both before and after implementation of the strategy — which balance considerations of management effectiveness, environmental impact, ease of implementation, and costs. Evaluation criteria for management strategies are discussed further in Chapter 10, *Record Keeping and Evaluations*.

CHAPTER SUMMARY

- PHC treatment recommendations must be timely and accurate. Practitioners must be aware of educational and formal training opportunities and know where and how to obtain the latest technical information.
- Extension advisors have pamphlets and brochures on key stresses for the locality, librarians will assist in computer searches for literature, and a compendium of PHC literature is available from professional tree care organizations.
- PHC provides alternative treatments:
  — cultural techniques often provide problem avoidance,
  — biological techniques can reduce pest populations,
  — chemical treatments may be required beyond threshold levels.
- Chemical treatment options include synthetic chemicals, horticultural soaps and oils, and natural chemicals such as pheromones and botanical toxins.
- Biological treatment options include multicellular and microbial organisms that prey on pests (parasites, predators, viruses), the toxins and other substances they produce that negatively impact pest behavior, and cover crops and mulches.

CHAPTER 10

Record Keeping and Evaluation

INTRODUCTION

> *Plant Health Care is an information-intensive operation.*

Plant Health Care, as emphasized many times before, is an ***information-intensive*** operation. The strategy balances management options from cultural, biological and chemical arenas only after careful examination of all factors relevant to each unique landscape situation. Each step of PHC program implementation is built on decisions made after accessing and considering information from outside resources (Chapter 9) and internal business records. The records quantify observations and results in concrete terms, and allow the business to improve and grow as a result of the practical lessons they provide. The scope and content of internal records necessary for PHC practice are outlined below.

For each landscape site under management, background data about the previous and current tree care practices and pesticide usage should be acquired. Unfortunately, the use of pesticides for ***amenity trees*** has not been well documented or assessed. For commercial or municipal properties, some information may be on formal record, or extrapolated from past budget accounts. For residential properties, these records may not be available (especially when the property has changed hands), and even property owners who have employed professional landscape care services in the past may not be aware of actual pesticides or practices used on their site. Any information the owner can supply about past landscape services can provide valuable insight into, for example, potential pesticide residues on site or past conditions that may have encouraged a current insect infestation or tree stress problem. For residential properties, municipal records (information about handling of street trees or other trees in the vicinity) are also valuable.

Once a PHC practitioner assumes responsibility for a property, specific site records are accumulated as detailed in Chapter 7 and below, along with any incidence of client complaint or inquiry regarding the management or condition of the property. Monitoring, and in particular the initial visits for site assessment and inventory, will give the PHC practitioner points of reference, ***baseline data*** for gauging progress from season to season, and a template for determining actual costs.

Some records (e.g., pesticide purchase records) may be logged in by office staff. Other essential records (e.g., treatment application records) might be first recorded on checklists during treatment visits, then transferred to a permanent file record. Standard (empty) **checklists** and **recording forms** should ideally be created and stored in a **microcomputer** in the office. This way, forms can be altered easily to meet new demands or needs, and new forms can be quickly printed when needed. The in-house record keeping should also be stored in a computer, which can be backed up with hardcopy files of the same information in looseleaf binders. Microcomputer-generated records (using an inventory or **database software**) are simple to access and available for immediate consultation. The files are most easily managed and compared when they can be handled in computer format.

TREATMENT RECORDS

> *Exacting records of all treatments used and plants treated are essential.*

Exacting records of all treatments used and plants treated are essential. This record keeping is a safety and protection measure, as well as an efficient tool for cost accounting and guiding evaluations for future treatments on a site.

Treatment records for each individual application situation should include all of the information illustrated in the checklist in Figure 10-1, including record of the pest problem (including species information or interaction between pest and environmental stress problem, if applicable), information on the exact location of the problem on the site, the time the problem is noted, duration of the problem, decision on when to begin treatment (may not be immediate, but may be delayed to coincide with the most vulnerable stage of an insect, for example), actual treatment applications and repeat applications, incidence of circumstances (e.g. unscheduled rainfall) that may interfere with treatment effectiveness.

Pesticide use should be noted with **dosages**, **formulations**, and **trade** and **generic names** included. Pesticides should be categorized in lists of herbicides, insecticides, fungicides, soil fumigants, and miscellaneous other chemicals (e.g. defoliants, rodent poisons). Dates of application are recorded along with details on costs, personnel and equipment required during the application. Time spent on treatment versus time spent on other landscape maintenance (including preventative measures) will be gauged during evaluations, using these records. All treatment records will be followed up with evaluations of treatment effectiveness.

Treatment checklists should be thorough and inclusive of all relevant information. Records for an individual PHC operation may be similar to the checklist in Figure 10-1, or be modified to suit the manager. However, it is important that all the records be standardized, in both format and process, since the records are only comparable if they consistently record the same facts. This continuity is best achieved by providing an actual, preprinted checklist to monitors or other staff taking records, to encourage collection of all appropriate data. The tangible standard information-gathering forms prompt more timely, consistent inspections, and concrete records of inspection results. All records for a particular site will be stored together, in chronological or reverse chronological order, to facilitate ready cross-referencing on the treatment history of the site. Checklists as in Figure 10-1 can be easily reproduced for recording the results of each site visit for treatment. Once transferred to a microcomputer record, the repeat applications can be logged on the same file with appropriate dates designated.

Treatment records are likely to reflect that some of the most demanding, **time-intensive** plant problems are associated with key plant/key stress complexes as described in Chapter 7. These combinations on a landscape site are

---

INTERNAL PESTICIDE APPLICATION RECORD

Treatment Record for _____
(client/site address identification)

1. Type of pest/problem _____
   (pest species/stage of development/population level/interaction with environmental conditions/secondary problems)

2. Location of pest on site _____
   (pinpointed location on the property/extent of the range)

3. Date of initial observation _____

   Date(s) of repeated observation _____

   Date when satisfactory control noted _____

4. Target date for treatment intervention _____

5. Treatment date _____

   Treatment strategy _____

   Pesticide used (if any) _____
   (name, EPA reg. no., active ingredient, formulation, rate)

   Other circumstances to be noted _____

   Applicators _____

Figure 10 - 1. Recommended minimum information to be included in a *pesticide application form.*

likely to demand repeated treatment, but should be useful in demonstrating advantages of an integrated PHC approach over repetitive pesticide applications that have been required in the past. Another related problem that might be reflected in treatment records is the tendency for old specimens, or trees that are stressed by urban environments and lack adequate resources, to gradually require increased treatment attention. Such specimens, even if not typically found on "key plant" lists, may suffer stress due to pavements that crowd root systems, or repeated, severe pruning to avoid competition with power lines. Even tree species that are relatively resilient may suffer sufficient stress under urban conditions to become susceptible to attack. Over time, these large, urban-stressed trees may demand more and more management time, and in extreme cases, their importance to the landscape might need to be evaluated against the maintenance requirements.

REGULATORY REQUIREMENTS

In order to satisfy legal requirements, additional, thorough records are required to document pesticide purchases, storage, and application. Figure 10-1 covers pesticide records specific to single treatment situations, including pesticide dosages, names (common and generic), **EPA reg. No.**, application times, etc. Other records relate to pesticide purchase, storage, and disposal, unrelated to specific treatment applications. These records are not only essential for legal protection of the PHC manager, but will be consulted for evaluations of cost

120 / THE PLANT HEALTH CARE MANAGEMENT SYSTEM

effectiveness and treatment effectiveness.

Records for pesticide purchase, storage and disposal are detailed in Figure 10-2. Pesticide purchases should be routinely, promptly documented with record of the pesticide name (trade and generic names), formulation, **active ingredient**(s), supplier, cost, and date of purchase. Pesticide storage records repeat some of this same information, but also include details on the condition of the material stored. Excess storage of unopened packets (out of season) will alert the PHC manager to adjust reorder projections. Partially-used packages in storage are susceptible to rodent or other damage. Dates of storage and dates of retrieval on record also aid in ordering projections and facilitate efficient use of materials in supply. Computer-printouts of this information may be protected in a plastic sleeve and stored with each lot of chemical for ready access. Pesticide disposal records again document name of product and other similar identification and date information specific to disposal of waste pesticides.

A PHC business will also be responsible for maintaining up-to-date routine health and work records, which clearly document any work (or treatment) related injuries, or days lost. Accidents due to **pesticide exposure** and resulting action/treatments are kept in the record as part of the permanent file. In order to provide maximum safety to employees, a PHC manager should periodically inspect the pesticide mixing facilities (Figure 10-3), to check availability of required safety equipment and organization of the area.

> *A PHC business will be responsible for maintaining up-to-date routine health and work records.*

ADDITIONAL RECORDS

Additional internal records in the PHC business program include specific customer records of site analysis, site inventory and diagnostic decisions that have previously been described (Chapters 7-9), as well as follow-up evaluation reports. Copies of client-specific contracts and custom-tailored reports and billings are also held on record for consultation and improvement of the PHC program.

FOLLOW-UP/EVALUATION

ACCURACY OF DIAGNOSIS/EFFECTIVENESS OF TREATMENT

Post-treatment evaluation visits are conducted using the same techniques described under monitoring visits (Chapter 7). The accuracy of diagnosis and effectiveness of treatment can be gauged by assessment of control, and comparison of site monitoring records before and after treatment measures were taken. Acceptable injury levels (thresholds) may be difficult to quantify consistently, prompting greater reliance on written observations and data to help direct management decisions on treatment effectiveness. Some treatments can be expected to demonstrate immediate effects/benefits for evaluation, whereas some alternative tactics may not show benefits until the following season (or thereafter). With follow-up evaluations of PHC programs, implementation procedures and future strategies are continually modified and fine-tuned. As monitoring data accumulates over a period of years, the predictive and planning capabilities of the PHC practitioner become increasingly more accurate.

Early evaluations are made as a follow-up to Record of Treatment forms (Figure 10-1). For example, for insect pest treatments, pest populations must be monitored after treatment to determine if populations have been checked below threshold, and to guard against resurgence of pests (rapid reestablish-

> *As monitoring data accumulates over a period of years, the predictive and planning capabilities of the PHC practitioner become increasingly more accurate.*

PESTICIDE PURCHASE LOG

PESTICIDE
Material purchased (trade and generic names):

Formulation:

Active ingredient:

EPA Reg. #:

Quantity:

Supplier:

Date of purchase:

Cost of material (including cost per unit a.i.):

PESTICIDE STORAGE
Material stored (trade and generic names):
- clearly labeled?

Formulation:

Active ingredient:

Quantity stored:

Condition:
- full or partially-used package?
- leaking container or bag?

Exact storage location:
- locked?
- ventilated?
- adequate lighting?

Date placed in storage:

Date(s) retrieved:

PESTICIDE DISPOSAL
Material discarded (trade and generic names):

Formulation:

Active ingredient:

Quantity discarded:

Transport to disposal site:

Name of employee disposing material:

Disposal site:

Contact information for disposal site:

Method of disposal:

Date of disposal:

Figure 10 - 2. Recommended content for a *Pesticide Purchase Log.*

CHEMICAL PREPARATION AREA CHECKLIST

Available safety equipment
☐ gloves   ☐ respirator
☐ goggles   ☐ aprons
☐ first aid supplies   ☐ hardhats
☐ boots   ☐ eyewash bottle

Emergency shower accessible/working order?
Separate, labeled measuring equipment for herbicides, insecticides, fungicides, and other materials?
Color coding?
Working scales?

Spill control materials
☐ broom   ☐ heavy plastic bags
☐ drip pans   ☐ shovel
☐ absorbent pillows   ☐ fire extinguisher/sand

Cleanliness of area?

Figure 10 - 3. Sample content for a *Chemical Preparation Area Checklist*.

> *Incidence of unanticipated hazards or treatment failures must be documented to avoid similar problems in the future.*

ment of populations after treatment). If, during repeat applications for the same pest problem, higher dosages or more frequent applications were required for effective management, it could indicate development of pest resistance in a population. Under these circumstances, alternative strategies must be developed to avoid further development of resistance. If a pesticide treatment was applied, the effects on natural enemy populations must further be assessed. While registrations (labels) give a fairly accurate indication of chemical effectiveness against a target pest, information about effects on non-target species may be unavailable (may require on-site evaluation).

Benefits of some cultural tactics can not be assessed so quickly after the measure is taken. For example, interior canopy pruning to increase aeration, eliminate weakened limbs that receive inadequate light, or make insect habitats less favorable can best be assessed in a subsequent year, once the tree has recovered from pruning wounds and any unwanted stimulation of waterspout emergence can be evaluated.

Final and interim evaluations will, in addition to the above, answer questions on whether or not objectives were achieved in reasonable time, and if side effects or damage related to treatment were observed.

Incidence of unanticipated hazards or treatment failures must be documented to avoid similar problems in the future. For example, cases where pests have eventually resurged and/or developed apparent resistance following chemical pesticide may provide valuable evidence in favor of more diverse, integrated strategies for future treatments. Errors in prediction or diagnosis may be the result of inadequate background knowledge of the pest biology. In this case, the evaluation should lead to better research or reference training on the pest/problem in question. Unexpected weather conditions might have contributed to error in prediction, or unanticipated changes in the overall ecology (biology/behavior of the natural predators of the pest). Each time these incidents are documented, the accuracy of future predictions or diagnosis is strengthened.

Incidence of public exposure to pesticides or outbreak of new, unanticipated pests (if the natural ecological balance has been disrupted) gives further evidence. Failures or disappointing results using PHC tactics must be documented as well, so that the strategies can be progressively modified and improved with experience.

COST EFFECTIVENESS

Plant Health Care can be extremely cost-effective. All impacts of the program, however, must be assessed during calculation of costs. It is useful to calculate and market in terms of ***cost/benefit analysis*** rather than just strict cost accounting as compared to conventional arboricultural services. Costs of conventional landscape management/treatment services are relatively easy to assess (in simple terms, costs of purchasing and applying chemicals). Costs of pesticides and applicator manpower should be greatly reduced when integrated tactics are used in place of traditional cover sprays. As an example documentation, the Davey Company reported outstanding savings/reductions in materials (insecticides) used in five test markets after adopting a plant health care strategy using soaps in combination with chemicals.

Transition to PHC will incur new sources of costs, not part of traditional cost accounting in the landscape care profession. New costs for monitoring will be realized, as well as substantial initial costs for training skilled PHC employees, program administration and record keeping, upgrades of equipment, and acquisition of relatively expensive biological control supplies. Using standard cost-accounting criteria, the actual costs for conducting any phase of a PHC program can be calculated as shown in Figure 10-4. Costs for administration, training, and record keeping are not included, but can be assessed using standard methods for indirect costs.

Cost assessment is not a simple matter of balancing the reduction in pesticide costs against the increased costs associated with PHC program implementation and development. Since one aim of PHC is to provide permanent solutions, not treatments that require repeat intervention, the cost effectiveness of PHC should be assessed over a long term, not just in initial years of implementation, when conversion costs are likely to be higher. Actual costs for PHC maintenance of each property should be reduced in years following initial implementation since early records (site inventory, map, etc.) can be quickly and efficiently updated in subsequent years. Adoption of more resistant plants and better site preparations and cultural practices will further reduce treatment costs in future years.

Reduction in chemical pesticide use, from an ecological rather than economic perspective and improved public attitudes and environmental conditions, although difficult to quantify, are factors beyond straight cost that need to be considered. Since PHC practices should prevent major devastating landscape problems from occurring, the aesthetic value of a landscape should be enhanced. While aesthetics are difficult to assess in terms of costs, improved landscape appearance and health are exactly the effects planned in any maintenance approach. Long-term economic and environmental effects, improved aesthetics, and increased client confidence and satisfaction are all factors that must be included in the cost assessment.

> *One aim of PHC is to provide permanent control solutions, not treatments that require repeat intervention*

COST EVALUATIONS OF TREATMENT

Pest/problem: _____
Site location: _____
Type of treatment or control tactic taken: _____
Date: _____
Repeat or alternative treatment strategies: _____
Date(s): _____
Components of cost: _____
- number of employee hours _____
- materials and supplies consumed _____
- equipment used/equipment hours _____

Total costs: _____
- Employee hours x wage scales   = _____
- cost of materials   = _____
- equipment hours x rate   = _____

TOTAL COST OF ACTIVITY   = _____

Figure 10 - 4. Sample *Cost Evaluation* form.

While PHC programs offer excellent potential for program expansion, very little concrete information on cost analysis is available. Clients who express willingness to limit chemical applications and alter traditional tree care methods must also commit funds to contract for additional PHC services.

SCHEDULE FOR FUTURE ACTION

To establish priorities for future action and to plan subsequent budgets, both the evaluation records and client satisfaction assessments must be considered. No management strategy for tree health is permanent, and while PHC leads to longer term, continuous health solutions as opposed to frequently repeated emergency treatments, new or repeat problems on a site can be expected. The diligent monitoring of a site, for example, is a 'future action' step that must be planned for any site, as it will be able to help predict onset of future problems rather than just force an arborist to react to unexpected disease or insect infestation. Similarly, management strategies which involved cultural steps (e.g. pruning, fertilization) can be scheduled for predictable repeat performance. Past records can help predict the probable need for return visits in other cases as well.

It is particularly critical to educate clients on the importance of scheduling for future monitoring and, when warranted, management measures. Clients with a well-maintained, problem-free landscape are well-advised that only continued PHC attention will guarantee future satisfaction.

Monitoring records will provide concrete, detailed evidence as to how successful management measures were, given actual numbers of site visits, rates and volumes of pesticide or other materials used, climate, and cultural practices. Samples taken before and after intervention will document PHC performance. When this data is logged on a computerized data base file, it is easy

> *Clients with a well-maintained, problem-free landscape are well-advised that only continued PHC attention will guarantee future satisfaction.*

to extract certain points and allow patterns or trends to become visible. These records guide future action for a particular landscape site, but further point out ways to improve accuracy or efficiency in future encounters of similar problems. For example, if a monitoring system failed to detect build-up of a damaging insect population before threshold level damage occurred, then the monitoring must occur more frequently, or the system of sampling and data collection should be redesigned.

CLIENT INFORMATION AND COMMUNICATION

Plant Health Care is such a complex management approach, relative to spray controls, and so different from conventional practices, that effective implementation will always require frequent communication and a degree of education of the client.

Fortunately, thorough explanations on the overall PHC strategy (see Compendium, as well as this manual) are available, and can be adapted by the arborist for communications with clients as needed. Ample current, updated scientific information about new perspectives and developments are readily available through Cooperative Extension Services, and agriculture departments in Land-Grant Institutions. Demonstration projects which illustrate the PHC approach in practice have been conducted in many urban and suburban areas by these institutions. Case histories of PHC "success stories" are documented and available for illustration. Dramatic reductions in the volume of chemical pesticides used on commercial and residential properties under PHC-type management systems have been repeatedly documented, and serve as excellent testimony in favor of this approach. Delivery systems for PHC programs have been developed by private consultants, extension agents, and universities.

PHC practitioners must take responsibility for delivery and translation of PHC principles into terms that allow each client to appreciate the personal benefits to be gained. Awareness of this unfamiliar approach should be fostered by using a variety of communication devices: written (newsletters, articles), visual (logos and symbols), oral (discussion sessions, guest lectures), and hands-on (school field trips, games, contests). Further opportunity for explaining PHC concepts to clients can occur during initial agreements for service (preparation of contracts and proposals) or as part of the routine business communications that occur during and after service (guarantees, reports, notices, or bills). In addition to these written communications, explanations and further education may occur during personal one-on-one discussions, or in handouts or leaflets, articles, lectures, letters, and more. Practitioners may elect to provide a loose-leaf PHC binder (with categorized sections) to clients for storage of and reference to the information leaflets, personalized written communications, and a copy of the landscape map since these will be useful in subsequent seasons.

> *Awareness of the PHC approach should be fostered by using a variety of communication devices...*

CONTRACTS/PROPOSALS

Simple, straightforward descriptions of the PHC philosophy and approach are communicated immediately to a new client in the contract/proposal. Succinct written statements emphasizing the environmentally-conscious nature of the approach, the safety, the sound scientific basis, and the benefits to the long-term health of plants are presented up front. This introduction must convey that the PHC strategy depends on the expertise of the professional practitioner, perhaps using strong, illustrative examples, but should never overwhelm the layman with details on the complexity of alternatives. Clients learn they are included in the process through ongoing monitoring reports, and can be active participants in the program.

Remember that long-term relationships are desired. Successful contracts and proposals for landscape maintenance are the prelude to long-term client relationships. An unsightly disease symptom or broken tree limb may have been the reason an arborist was called to the property, but the focus as a PHC practitioner will be on complete health care for the entire landscape environment. Thorough estimates for providing PHC services on a property can only logically be prepared after a tree inventory and initial monitoring survey have been completed.

These critical steps in initiating a PHC program should not be provided gratis, but should be clearly included in the initial fee to a potential long-term client. A charge for preliminary monitoring allows the PHC practitioner to conduct a thorough, meaningful analysis of requirements for a site, without an unnecessary financial risk, if a continued contract with the client is not obtained. Site inventory and monitoring demand special expertise and training and are labor intensive. This should be reflected in a standard fee which emphasizes to the potential client the essential nature of these information-gathering steps to a comprehensive landscape health care program.

After the first monitoring site visit, a practitioner can provide an estimate for services. The estimate may focus on the specific service requested by the client (e.g., treatment for a weakened tree that has been infested with aphids). But the PHC practitioner can further take the opportunity to detail, on a contract/proposal, a comprehensive series of maintenance procedures to maintain a property. A thorough, complete PHC program for any site will likely involve service components the typical client did not expect. For example, a client may be prepared to purchase treatments and perhaps some landscape maintenance services, but may be reluctant to contract for a regular monitoring service and preventative steps towards invigorating landscape plants. In these cases, the program may need to be initially streamlined to balance the requirements of the plants and the price-resistance of the client. The visible benefits of the PHC program will be evident to each client as the program continues, and satisfaction will encourage adoption of the complete program package in subsequent years.

The PHC contract/proposal will provide a description of maintenance plans for the site, based on the monitor's assessment visit. Each procedure, and its justification, can be individually itemized. This individualized assessment may be described first in letter form (Figure 10-5), reporting the findings of the monitor and detailing management measures the PHC program will take to maintain the property. The client may opt to select only part of a program, but few would even consider the benefits of a comprehensive PHC program without this initial estimate and plan from the practitioner. The client must also be convinced during discussion of the proposal that PHC can only be successful when the plants are given adequate maintenance to ensure excellent health. A professionally-designed PHC program with realistic goals for success must be thorough and long term. For example, a single treatment to manage a pest infestation will only afford temporary benefit, whereas repeated follow-up with additional cultural steps to increase tree vigor are likely to maintain lasting tree health.

Once agreement has been reached with the client, a detailed contract will be submitted, detailing trees and shrubs to be monitored, and cultural modifications to be employed on the property, dates of future service scheduled in advance, and price (Figure 10-6).

> *A thorough, complete PHC program for any site will likely involve service components the typical client did not expect.*

(to be prepared on company letterhead)

Date

Client Address   Service Address

Dear Mr. ——

In response to your call on [April 12, 1995], we have recently completed a monitoring inspection and inventory of your property at —— Street, ——. We in particular investigated the cause behind the unsightly appearance of the two mature Tuliptrees in your front yard, as you requested.

We discovered that the Tuliptrees were infested with a species of aphid, which is damaging the leaves and creating the sticky "honeydew" residue around your front patio (see label A on the attached map of your property). We plan to control this problem with a combination of a low concentration of Orthane (a specific, recommended pesticide) combined with insecticidal soap. This procedure has proven to be extremely effective against aphid problems in this area. In addition, these two trees should be carefully pruned to preserve the structure of the canopy, but to allow more light and air to penetrate the tree. This procedure will increase the vitality of the trees, and make the interior canopy less susceptible to future attacks of the insect.

We observed an additional need for pruning of the Burning bush hedge in your back yard (see label B on the attached map), which is obstructing traffic near the sidewalk, and recommend mulching on your exposed planting beds throughout the yard to cut down on weed problems and conserve moisture around your plants. In order to ensure uninterrupted good health and excellent appearance of your landscape long term, we propose a series of 4 inspection visits to your property this year, at timed intervals, to monitor the effectiveness of these procedures, catch any new problems before they develop, and recommend any further action.

The individualized landscape health care plan we've designed for your landscape is detailed on the attached proposal. The estimated schedule for monitoring visits is spaced throughout the growing season. In addition, we will keep you informed of our progress throughout the season, and provide you with a detailed year-end summary to thoroughly explain the improvements which will occur on your property. Please do not hesitate to call us if you have any further questions. Thank you for the chance to prepare this assessment for you, and we look forward to the task of caring for your landscape.

Thank you!

Figure 10 - 5. Example of a *Contract/Proposal Letter* to client.

REPORTS

In PHC, the client is kept up-to-date on the analysis of field monitors, and will be promptly informed of decisions made and action taken on his/her property through reports. A synopsis report for client information can be abstracted from information accumulated by the monitor and recorded on the monitor checklist. Figure 10-7 illustrates a simple condition report that will be presented to the client promptly after each monitoring visit. The date of the next monitoring visit should be clearly indicated on this form, as shown.

A summary of the year's activities on a property is an excellent means for establishing rapport with clients, and introducing some principles of PHC. A year-end summary will clearly recap the progressive, planned steps taken during maintenance of a site (Figure 10-8). The summary can be an effective device to demonstrate how cultural practices (such as fertilization, or mulching) actu-

Detailed Contract for Service

Landscape Plant Health Maintenance Proposal - (Year)

Client:

Work address: Home Address:

Business phone: Home Phone:

Monitor ID:

Date of Inspection:

Tuliptree Treatment:
(Horticultural Oil and Pesticide Application; Interior Canopy Pruning)

    Price =

Additional maintenance needs:

Pruning of hedges:

Mulching all beds:

    Price =

Complete health maintenance plan, including monitoring visits on your property, periodic reports, and a final end of year evaluation to assess improvements.

    Total annual cost =

Figure 10 - 6. Sample *Contract for Service* form.

PHC — Periodic Monitor Report

Date of Scheduled Monitoring Visit:

Client Identification:

Account Number:

Inspector(s):

Specific Activities/Observations:

Recommendations/Course of Action:

Figure 10 - 7. Sample *Periodic Monitor Report* form.

PHC—End-of-Year Program Summary

Date: _____

Client Identification: _____

Account Number: _____

Inspector(s): _____

Summary of Tree Health Management goals and accomplishments for 19—:
_____
_____

Recommendations for next season's maintenance of your property:
_____
_____

Figure 10 - 8. Suggested content for an *End-of-Year Program Summary*.

ally fit into the integrated PHC strategy, as tools to invigorate plants and avoid stress. Finally, a year-end summary demonstrates the continuous, ongoing process required for an effective management system, and can be an excellent means to encourage repeated contracts with the client.

NOTICES/INSERTS

Individual explanatory brochures covering topics that tie together the PHC approach, including principles of landscape inventory and mapping, the role of cultural practices in tree health, pest management strategies, or the purpose of monitoring are examples of useful topics for short, informative pamphlets which can help clients embrace the concept of PHC. Specific facts sheets, which focus on selected problems or concerns, may be distributed to clients when relevant.

Pesticide awareness fact sheets provide crucial information to allay client fears about even limited pesticide applications performed in PHC programs, and can be supplied to those clients who express concerns. These fact sheets can document the safety and environmentally-conscious approach taken in the program. They further give evidence of well-planned, technically solid decision making made by the PHC practitioner regarding pesticide use.

> *Pesticide awareness fact sheets provide crucial information to allay client fears.*

Research has shown that clients have a very positive response to additional information provided (see Chapter 2). It can also help build personal communications with a client. For example, if the practitioner should learn by chance a client has a particular interest in hummingbirds, an occasional pamphlet on hummingbirds or lists of plants that attract hummingbirds could accompany other mailed materials.

Teach the client to, at least in part, recognize PHC principles and use these diverse strategies on their own. Some communities, in concert with university or extension specialists, have instituted homeowner educational programs/courses with this goal in mind. This is important, since clients (especially residential homeowners) may elect to hire landscape care professionals for some site care functions, but wish to handle other tasks in the landscape on their own. Educational aids can guide these home gardeners in wise selection of resistant plants, simple identification of damaging pests, and cultural practices that can supplement the professional's practices. Hopefully, the client will freely seek professional advice or service for more complex aspects of the PHC approach. Instead of taking business away from the professional PHC practitioner, research surveys have indicated that informed homeowners are more willing to contract for commercial services.

PHC companies can strengthen the positive message conveyed by the PHC approach by visibly supporting other related environmental issues, such as Earth Day, or the American Forester's Global ReLeaf Program. These clearly environmental campaigns reinforce the importance of trees to the world, and bolster support for complete, sound programs that foster tree health without disrupting the ecosystem. Facts and written materials provided through these concerns can tie into the bulletins or newsletters provided to the client by the PHC company, to the benefit of both.

BILLINGS/SERVICE EVALUATIONS

Plant Health Care emphasizes client participation in the landscape maintenance plan. The PHC practitioner regularly submits reports and evaluations to the client after service. As a logical adjunct to this philosophy, the client must further have the opportunity to evaluate the service of the PHC practitioner (Figure 10-9). After services have been performed, and as billing is submitted, clients are asked to give their impression and voice their satisfaction/dissatisfaction with the program and results. This follow-up request demonstrates to each client that their satisfaction is important, and their opinions valued. In addition, the **Service Evaluation Survey** is a tool that can be used to assess the needs of clients and refine the PHC approach for subsequent seasons.

GUARANTEES

> *Confidence in the PHC strategy should be expressed by the consumer in a signed contract and by the arborist in a guarantee.*

A PHC program requires contact with the client by an informed arborist. Confidence in the PHC strategy should be expressed by the consumer in a signed contract and by the practitioner in a guarantee. The guarantee can be direct and simply stated. The guarantee should express in writing exactly what will be delivered. It should assure the client that the service delivered was the correct treatment applied at a suitable time with the recommended materials, dosage and equipment in order to attain the desired results within a reasonable time frame.

A guarantee assures that no other professional could have performed the service in a manner more satisfying to the client. The guarantee does not state that the problem will be solved, but that the most up-to-date, recommended practices were applied in a timely and professional manner. You guarantee customer satisfaction.

A client satisfaction guarantee by the practitioner is binding. PHC practitioners should be confident that their information and procedures will not be challenged by their peers, professional consultants, extension agents or university scientists. PHC practitioners will be in constant communication with these individuals to be assured that they can live up to the guarantee. Certification, attendance at educational conferences and membership in professional organizations is almost essential for PHC arborists.

Service Evaluation
(to be prepared on company letterhead)

Billing - Page 1
Service Evaluation - Page 2

Client identification/address information/account number (preprinted)   Date

Service Evaluation Survey

Please take a few minutes to give us your evaluation of the landscape maintenance plan conducted on your property by ———.

Your response will help us to continue to improve our PHC programs for our clients.

Evaluation of plant maintenance services:

Were you satisfied with the control of pests and problems on your plants? _____
_____
_____

Were clean-up operations prompt and thorough? _____
_____

Were you satisfied with the improved appearance of your property after service? _____
_____

How prompt were our employees in response to your request(s)? _____
_____
_____
_____

Figure 10 - 9. Sample *Service Evaluation* form to accompany billing statement as page 2.

CHAPTER SUMMARY

- Standardized, computerized, in-house records are the basis for monitoring and evaluating your business and the PHC services it provides.
- Desirable records include background data at each site, monitoring data (particularly from initial visits for site assessment and inventory), details of all treatments used and the plants treated, and observations from post-treatment site evaluations. Standardized formats and check-list forms facilitate collection of information and its computer entry.

- Record keeping must be extensive and thorough; it is a safety and protection mechanism, a tool for efficient cost accounting, and a guide for evaluating future treatments at a site.
- PHC clients desire contact, information, and aesthetics. Accurate records, ongoing evaluation processes, and the reports generated provide an informed foundation for frequent and sustained client interactions. Involve clients in your PHC program.

CHAPTER 11

PHC Equipment and Staffing

INTRODUCTION

> *... some experts have predicted that only arborists offering preventative tree health care programs (PHC) will survive in upcoming years.*

Given escalating insurance liabilities for pesticide applications and increased environmental consciousness on the part of urban clients, some experts have predicted that only arborists offering preventative tree health care programs (PHC) will survive in upcoming years. Once a business has committed to begin a PHC program, the transition may not be immediate. As stated earlier, maximum benefits and profits over the long term are produced when *all* PHC principles are applied. A complete PHC-based operation will offer each of the services outlined in this manual (monitoring, inventory, diagnosis, and diversified management strategies). However, the implementation and promotion of limited PHC services can be gradually built into existing services.

Individual enterprises with limited resources may find it necessary to begin implementation of a PHC program by first offering limited service(s) (e.g. monitoring and consultation). Several years of coordinated effort may go into the acquisition of new equipment and supplies, training of qualified staff, collection of local background information (on site history, key stresses, weather patterns, etc.), development and expansion of services, and developing the local market. Initial experience with limited PHC services may help the practitioner evaluate the potential client base and its willingness to contract for these newer concepts. It should be noted that a limited PHC program may be more difficult to sell than the full scope of services.

UPGRADE OF EQUIPMENT AND STAFF (FIELD AND OFFICE)

In a Plant Health Care enterprise, the appearance of equipment and the image projected by field employees must both be consistent with the ideals of a PHC program. Equipment must be in excellent condition, clean, and outfitted for flexibility in management options. Staff members must be well-versed in PHC principles, knowledgeable and articulate, able to interact well with clients, and able to diagnose plant problems and make informed treatment decisions.

PHC focuses on treatments rather than sprays. Treatments emphasize prevention of problems and manipulations of cultural conditions to promote plant health, and use of chemical treatments as a last-resort option. In agreement with this philosophy, PHC vehicles and the image projected by field employees during customer communications must also emphasize this focus.

For maximum efficiency and profit, PHC vehicles should be designed and equipped to fit each company and the type of clients it serves. For small companies or service to small residential properties, it may be more efficient for all steps of a PHC program to be completed by one or two highly paid and thoroughly trained employees with one fully equipped vehicle. For practitioners with larger client bases or larger properties, vehicle and employee functions may be more specialized. Specialization may increase the number of trips required to a property, and may require more employees and documentation. However, cost savings are possible because training is more concentrated, and employees can become more efficient. Decisions of this nature are dependent entirely on the goals and clientele of an individual business.

EQUIPMENT

> *PHC vehicle appearance must be highly professional.*

Basic equipment requirements for the PHC program include vehicles and control/maintenance equipment (including spray and related equipment).

VEHICLES:

Basic PHC vehicles include pick-up trucks outfitted with tree rigs, with mounted, locked cargo bins and mounted, locked water tanks with hose. Vehicles must be equipped with fire extinguishers.

Vehicle appearance must be highly professional. A client's initial impression of the PHC professional may be based on long-distance observation of the vehicle parked curbside or nearby. For this reason, vehicles of recent vintage should be maintained. All visible aspects of the vehicle (paint job, body work, storage cabinets, equipment and tool covers, and advertising signs) should be in first-class condition. Storage cabins reinforce a positive perception when organized, neat, clean, and clearly labeled. These directives are based on the image a PHC professional must maintain, but in fact, these details also confer a high degree of professional organization. This organization benefits the business in terms of efficiency and creates an enhanced image for the company and tree care industry as a whole.

SPRAY (AND RELATED) EQUIPMENT:

Pesticide application equipment designed for PHC practitioners allows mixing of specific chemicals in volumes of one to 150 gallons, with a separate freshwater tank and smaller pesticide mix tanks. This specialized equipment allows specific, targeted pesticide applications to be mixed and applied on a site, without waste and disposal of excess materials. For versatility, the PHC program should have available:
- a power hydraulic sprayer with adjustable jet nozzle
- a back-pack pump sprayer
- hand-held small (1-2 gallon) pump sprayers
  (Spray equipment should be secured to trucks with locks.)
- Clearly graduated measuring containers and utensils and plastic jars should be on hand
- Protective equipment necessary for safety during chemical applications includes eye goggles, shielded hard hat, respirator, rubber gloves, rain gear, hand soap and disposable towels, and first aid kit
- For clean-up of chemical spills, the following is needed: small shovels, push brooms, garbage bags, absorbent materials.

Other equipment and supplies:
- Pole saw, pole pruner, hand pruners, and rake
- Fertilizers and chemicals
- Pheromone traps (as appropriate to the area)
- Field copies of key reference books, for insect, disease, and plant identification
- Reporting forms (monitoring)
- Monitoring tools

STAFFING

Professional Plant Health Care employees will require enhanced educational training and skills required for monitoring. Personnel training and access to resource information is crucial. Figure 11-1 illustrates a personnel data form, which can be abstracted from employment contracts/resumes, and updated as the staff member continues with the PHC business. Especially for larger operations, these forms will aid the PHC manager to identify staff members most adapted/well-trained for complex PHC decision making, versus employees who have less management potential.

As noted in Chapter 2, the typical client for PHC services appreciates timely information about strategies used in his/her landscape. To keep these clients satisfied, the PHC field employee must maintain a positive interaction. The monitor or technician will be performing diagnosis and making strategy decisions and will most likely be the individual interacting with clients to educate on PHC principles. These individuals must have an inherent appreciation for trees and motivation towards maintaining tree health. Formal training in landscape horticulture, plant pathology, entomology and urban forestry are excellent qualifications. Employees need additional training in effective customer service, communications, and problem resolution. In-house educational programs for new employees may also be required. These training programs are an effective way to demonstrate, to both staff and clients, a business commitment to professional knowledge in the care of landscape plants. In many cases, qualified field employees will be able to circumvent problems if they can listen attentively to client concerns and be able to provide prompt professional answers.

To facilitate rapport between client and field employee, uniforms that include company name and logo, and that identify the employees by name are useful. Uniforms must be rigorously maintained to be kept neat and clean. In addition, field employees must be supplied with printed information on the PHC program and related topics. These brochures and pamphlets help reinforce professional consultations, and increase the client's awareness of PHC objectives in a positive sense.

> *The typical client for PHC services appreciates timely information about strategies used in his landscape.*

PROGRAM EXPANSION

Development of strong PHC programs must start with rigorous program planning and collection of required background information, as emphasized above. The objectives and scope of the initial PHC program must be outlined. Predictions and plans for expansion are made to facilitate allocation of funds over the transition period. Other relevant questions (e.g., "What will customer reactions be?," "Should initial client resistance be anticipated?," "How can current information be accessed quickly?") usually require research (in the form of litera-

PERSONNEL DATA FORM

Name: _____

Contact information (home and office): _____

Education: _____

Previous experience: _____

_____

_____

_____

Additional on-the-job training (attendance at pest management seminars or short courses): _____

_____

_____

Date hired: _____

Initial job title: _____

Present job title (date): _____

_____

Pesticide certification: _____

_____

Special service or recognition in the green industry: _____

_____

_____

_____

Citations or complaints regarding this staff member (or work completed by this staff member): _____

_____

_____

_____

Figure 11 - 1. Recommended *Personnel Data Form* information.

PHC EQUIPMENT AND STAFFING / 137

ture searches or client questionnaires) to assess the potential pitfalls and high points of a new business approach. In the case of PHC, many of these initial questions were already addressed in Chapter 2 and most current sources of information will be regularly available through the related Compendium. Specifically, survey results from current residential clients of tree care firms indicate that, in spite of recent environmental publicity, many homeowners do accept blanket pesticide spraying on their properties. These clients are also hesitant to contract for expanded PHC services that cost more than traditional services. Managers of commercial properties were more receptive to a PHC approach, as they recognize hazards (and liabilities) of pesticide overuse. This background information reinforces the need for PHC practitioners (managers and staff) to be well-versed in the principles and multiple benefits of the approach, and technically well-trained, to overcome reservations of potential clients. Background information about prevailing client misconceptions (concerning tree maintenance practices) allows retailored PHC programs to focus on overcoming these misconceptions. Employees require enhanced training to understand and implement PHC tactics, and clients require education (often via these employees) to be persuaded to contract for PHC.

> *Employees require enhanced training to understand and implement PHC tactics, and clients require education to be persuaded to contract for PHC.*

Local information (pertinent over the entire business area) is collected on site specifics, historic information, climate, and prioritization of typical pest problems, before any specific client problems are dealt with using PHC methods. Important sources of reference information are located, and systematically cataloged to allow quick access. Some key references may be purchased by the business, and sources for on-loan or no-charge updated information are established (library, cooperative extension service, local university, etc.). For maximum utility, the reference file should be cross-indexed by keyword, pest, plant, or other useful information (determined by the PHC manager). This is further justification for compiling the reference catalogue on an easy to access, microcomputer-based file.

In addition to the outside references and resources (which amounts to a wealth of information), an abstracted file of the most frequently encountered stress situations should be prepared for quick reference by staff members. This organized resource subfile, in summary form, should include concise information about each key stress, identification key features, biology of pests and their natural enemies, techniques for monitoring, and alternative management measures

An example of an abstracted file is shown in Figure 11-2. With on-the-job PHC program experience, the most effective combination(s) of management tactics in the area can be documented by PHC practitioners. This will yield an extremely valuable and relevant point of reference whenever the same problem is encountered again. Pictures or drawings to aid in identification may be included in the reference file. When appropriate, citations may be indexed on the abstracted summary file for study of more in-depth information about a pest or its plant host from outside reference materials. Compilation and frequent updating of this abstracted pest/problem resource file provide a more manageable quick resource (than the formidable information base available through outside literature). Its structure and maintenance also provide valuable training for staff members to develop monitoring expertise.

In-house training is initiated to prepare staff personnel for new responsibilities. Once the PHC program is initiated, new techniques are tested when appropriate, and evaluations of management and costs will guide the further development, modification, and fine-tuning of the expanding PHC program. Research conducted formally or informally during the course of business operations are crucial tools for improving future on-the-job performance.

ABSTRACTED PEST/PROBLEM RESOURCE FILE

Pest/problem identification [name, id features, hosts, geographic origin]:

Biology of pest (for biotic organisms):

[Overwintering (stage or site)]:

[Information on egg deposition sites, larval stage feeding, adult stage feeding, seasons for feeding and mating, and generations per year for insect pests]:

Biology of natural enemies or biotic controls:

List of techniques for monitoring:

Alternative management measures:

    Preventive/Avoidance management:

    Treatment intervention:

        Cultural:

        Biological:

        Chemical:

Effective combinations of above tactics:

Identification photographs or pictures:

Additional references:

Figure 11-2. Sample *Abstracted Pest/Problem Resource File*.

In the course of program expansion, new sources of PHC supplies (in particular, biological control supplies) must be established. The PHC alternatives for stress management have been outlined in the preceding chapters, but the practical and economic availability of some products is not optimum. Outside consultants are required for some of the aspects of business (for example, complex diagnosis tasks, or licensed release of biological controls), and vendors of PHC-related supplies may provide guidance in some cases. Diagnostic labs are available through universities, the USDA service, or extension services. These resources must also be sought and established. A reference card file of technical specialists and suppliers should be compiled including the name, contact information, area of specialization/product(s), and consultation fee (dated).

CHAPTER SUMMARY

- The full implementation of PHC services may require new equipment and supplies, additional staff training, collection of locality information, changes in business services offered, and market development. Specific equipment needs will vary with marketing strategies.
- PHC programs are benefitted by: employees who understand the principles of PHC and possess good communication skills and enhanced technical knowledge; by field manuals that describe alternate treatment methods; and by continuing modifications and fine-tuning of the program.

CHAPTER 12

PHC and the Landscape Design/Build Process

INTRODUCTION

While the Plant Health Care Management System has much to offer arborists in their care of trees and other landscape plants, it has equal value to landscape design/build professionals. The ultimate goal of PHC is "integrated landscape care" — a comprehensive, multi-dimensional strategy. Past plant care efforts focused attention on individual plants and unfortunately, often only on the above-ground portions of these plants. Effectiveness of plant care increases, however, as the size of the management unit goes from a single plant to the entire landscape. Effectiveness also increases when all landscape management professionals whose activities can influence the health and appearance of a plant focus their efforts within the framework of PHC. Selection of plant materials and their placement are determined by a landscape design/build company. Turf grass in the landscape is cared for by a lawn care company and their cultural treatments such as fertilizing and herbicide applications influence the health of trees and shrubs. Arborists contracted to care for trees must work within these previously set limitations. Each professional has an important role to play in the long-term care of the tree. It takes the integrated efforts of all these professionals — landscape architects and designers, landscape contractors, lawn maintenance specialists and arborists, to provide an effective systems approach to plant health management.

The foundation of the PHC approach is to optimize plant defense systems. Among other things, this can often reduce pesticide usage. Many of the most serious insect and disease organisms that affect the health of trees and other landscape plants are only *part* of the contributing factors in a plant's decline. Predisposing factors, such as climate, soils and the plant's genetic capacity to resist strain, are long-term factors that can compromise a plant's ability to adequately defend itself. These factors, in combination with inciting factors, such as droughts and defoliation, can further stress a plant and increase the probability of successful insect or disease colonization. Landscape architects and designers can fulfill a crucial role in the PHC system by selecting plants that have the genetic capacity to thrive in urban settings and matching the site to a particular plant's ecological requirements. Numerous plant failures can be ulti-

> *Many of the most serious insect and disease organisms that affect the health of trees and other landscape plants are only part of the contributing factors in a plant's decline.*

mately traced back to planting on a site to which the plant is poorly adapted. In addition, many plant health problems can be attributed to improper planting or neglected after-care. Landscape design/build companies can play a key role in Plant Health Care by minimizing the influence of these predisposing and inciting factors.

The concept of low-input, sustainable landscapes, such as xeriscapes, has become popular in the last decade. Sustainable landscapes can maintain themselves without an excessive influx of resources. In a recent survey of landscape architects, water availability was listed as the most important factor affecting plant selection. Also considered important by the group were plants that required less maintenance, and in particular, fewer pesticide applications. Garden center customers are also aware that careful attention to matching plants and sites pays off in lower maintenance cost. A recent survey of garden center customers showed that their most important information need was knowing the environmental conditions necessary for a particular plant to thrive. Plant Health Care is an important part of this new approach to landscape design and installation.

Plant Health Care can also be a marketing tool for the landscape design/build profession. Sustainable landscapes are becoming increasingly important considerations for many potential clients. They realize that the initial appearance of a newly installed landscape can be deceiving. Improperly designed or installed landscapes can quickly deteriorate leaving the client dissatisfied with the project and faced with higher replacement and maintenance costs. Not surprisingly, the larger the proposed landscape, the greater the client's concern about the viability of the plants being installed. Plant Health Care begins with selecting plant materials that are adapted to the site. This, in turn, helps to minimize the need for pesticides and other treatments to maintain their health. Equally important, PHC can be a means of positioning a company, conveying that their design and installation efforts are focused on the sustainability of the landscapes.

> *Sustainable landscapes are becoming increasingly important considerations... improperly designed or installed landscapes can quickly deteriorate leaving the client dissatisfied with the project...*

INCORPORATING PHC INTO THE DESIGN PROCESS

One of the first steps in the landscape design process is conducting a design analysis. This step consists of both a site analysis and a survey of the client's needs and desires. Generally the site analysis focuses on the functional and aesthetic features of a landscape. It is an assessment of the legal and physical characteristics of the property. The property dimensions are determined and buildings are located within it. The architectural style of the residential or commercial building is noted as well as the general features of the terrain. The site analysis also identifies good views to expose or frame along with gathering information on many other features. While soil and climate information is essential to the creation of a sustainable landscape, it is often simplified in the site analysis to merely identifying the hardiness zone in which the property is located and a quick check of soil texture. A PHC site analysis includes defining the physical characteristics of the landscape, but also includes a thorough environmental analysis of the site.

The foundation of a PHC design is properly matching site characteristics with plant ecological requirements. Landscape architects and designers routinely match plants to design criteria; size, form, texture and color. In PHC-based designs, this criteria is expanded to include environmental factors. Once an environmental analysis has been completed for a site and the design is completed, plants can be selected that fit the appropriate form, texture and color as well as match the site conditions for a particular location.

The environmental requirements for growth vary considerable among plant species. While many plants can adapt to a wide range of sites, each has its optimum range — sites in which environmental stresses are minimized and the plant is at a competitive advantage. Landscape architects and designers need to consider three broad categories of environmental factors; climate, soil and exposure when matching sites and plants.

Macro- and microclimates are important environmental factors to consider when selecting plants. However, many times only minimum winter temperature is considered. Summer mean temperature, fluctuations in fall and spring temperatures and precipitation, both annual and growing season, are all important climate characteristics. Balsam fir (*Abies balsamea*), for example, is considered to be an extremely cold hardy tree, but its ornamental use is limited due to its intolerance of July mean temperature above 18 C (65 F). Even the hardiness zone map's reliance on minimum winter temperature is misleading. Cold hardiness needs to be based upon more than midwinter hardiness; the rate of acclimation and deacclimation should be considered as well. Norway maple (*Acer platanoides*) is one of the most common ornamental trees, but can experience winter injury in the northern region of the United States. Some cultivars have been successful, not because of their ability to tolerate lower midwinter temperatures (many Norway maple cultivars tolerate midwinter temperatures of -30 C (-22 F)), but because they acclimate earlier in the fall and deacclimate later in the spring, thus are less affected by the wide temperature fluctuations that can occur during these seasons.

Landscape architects and designers need to develop plant palettes for the individual markets they serve. Plant materials should be categorized not only by hardiness zones, but by summer temperatures and precipitation ranges as well as tolerance to spring and fall temperature fluctuations. Obviously, while plants collected from local sources are adapted to the climate, plants from similar climates can also do well. Plant palettes identifying only species that come from similar climates are not the complete solution. Many trees have large natural ranges that may cover several different climates. Red maple (*Acer rubrum*), for example, is native from northern Minnesota to southern Florida. Red maple cultivars selected from one part of this range may not be adapted to another part. 'Northwood' red maple, a seedling selection from northern Minnesota performs well in northern regions while 'October Glory' an east central U.S. selection does well in southern states. Landscape architects and designers should compile lists of species and cultivars that can adapt to the local climate.

Soil factors are also important considerations. Many plants can be climatically adapted to a particular region, but may not tolerate the prevailing soils. One of the most common problems experienced in urban areas is planting in clay soils. These soils, in addition to having poor drainage, are also often alkaline due to the lime present in the soil or from run off from concrete and limestone surfaces. Even in areas with naturally acidic soils, it is not uncommon to have alkaline soils occurring near buildings and paved areas. Soil pH needs to be determined in two key planting areas, near foundations and in lawn areas. If a great variation is noted between several samples within these areas, more planting sites may need to be sampled to define the range of pHs occurring in a site. If the site or sites are determined to be alkaline, calciphytes such as Shumard oak (*Quercus shumardii*) and other species that tolerate alkaline soils, should be planted. Environmental analysis should also include an examination of the soil profile to ascertain variability. Soils in areas developed after the

> *While many plants can adapt to a wide range of sites, each has its optimum range — sites in which environmental stresses are minimized and the plant is at a competitive advantage.*

> *Many plants can be climatically adapted to a particular region, but may not tolerate the prevailing soils.*

1940's are often highly disturbed and bear little resemblance to the natural soil profile. Such soils may be poorly drained as water movement is interrupted by extreme and abrupt changes in soil texture. Variation can be sampled by using a soil auger to collect samples throughout the planting area to a depth of two to three feet. Soils having poor drainage may need to have tiling or plant selection limited to species that can tolerate these adverse conditions. Floodplain species are generally adapted to the wet soils during the spring and are also tolerant of dry soils during the summer. Two common floodplain species, green ash (*Fraxinus pennsylvanica*) and silver maple (*Acer saccharinum*) are popular choices for poorly drained soils.

Exposure is also an important consideration when matching plants to a particular location. Plants species do not usually occur randomly within a climate or soil type. Some species will be found growing in full sun while others thrive beneath the canopy of taller trees. Foresters often refer to this phenomenon as shade tolerance — the ability of a plant to grow within the shade of other trees. Certain species such as sugar maple (*Acer saccharum*) and beech (*Fagus grandifolia*) are considered extremely shade tolerant and can grow in deep shade, while quaking aspen (*Populus tremuloides*) and cottonwood (*Populus deltoides*) are shade intolerant and only thrive in full sun. Ignoring the light requirements of plants can lead to transplant failure. Shade intolerant trees such as thornless honeylocust (*Gleditsia triacanthos* var. *inermis*) are sometimes planted beneath the canopies of larger trees. These honeylocust often grow slowly and are predisposed to colonization by disease organisms. Planting shade tolerant understory trees and shrubs in open sites can also be an environmental stress and increase pest problems. Plants need to be carefully matched with the light intensities for a particular site. Empirically determined shade tolerance plant lists have been created and these lists are useful guides for choosing plants for a particular location.

While light intensity is a major factor in determining placement, it is necessary that it be considered with other factors such as temperature as well. Paper birch (*Betula papyrifera*) is classified as shade intolerant within much of its natural range. However, it does not tolerate high soil or air temperatures. Along the southern extreme of its range, paper birch is generally restricted to north-facing slopes. The cool, moist microclimate along these slopes provides a better environment for temperature sensitive birches. Birch placed in a sunny lawn area of the central United States are stressed by high air and soil temperatures. In such planting, the need for cool temperatures outweighs the need for sunlight and birch does best along the north sides of buildings.

In addition to properly matching plants to particular site conditions, it is also essential that only healthy plants be placed into the landscape and that installation be conducted properly. There are numerous guides available on the subjects of selecting plants from nurseries and proper transplanting techniques for installation of bare root, container, balled & burlapped and tree spaded plants.

> *In addition to properly matching plants to particular site conditions, it is also essential that only healthy plants be placed into the landscape and that installation be conducted properly.*

MARKETING PHC LANDSCAPES

Plant Health Care can be a valuable marketing tool for design/build professionals. Plant Health Care can be used to position a company and provide a unique approach to selling design fees, landscape installations and landscape warranties.

Many landscape design/build companies no longer provide "free" designs for residential clients, but instead charge a design fee of $75 - $450 to prepare a landscape plan. Some companies will credit the fee towards the installation price if the client chooses to have the plan implemented. Other companies charge a design fee regardless the client's decision regarding installation. Selling a design fee is a difficult task for many designers. Most markets have many landscape companies that are willing to prepare landscape plans at no charge merely on speculation that the client may approve of their plan and proceed with installation. Preparing a residential landscape plan requires about eight to twelve hours in many design/build companies when the time for the one or two client meetings, design analysis and landscape plan and take-off sheets is totaled.

The time required to prepare a landscape plan represents a valuable resource and compensation is reasonable and an accepted practice for many similar professions. One barrier to charging a design fee is the client's perceived value of the design process. Many view designing as the simple task of decorating their outdoor living area. They rarely appreciate the knowledge required to create a sustainable landscape that increases in value with time. To overcome this sales barrier, companies that charge a design fee identify, in a design contract, the various time-consuming tasks that are performed in the preparation of a thorough landscape plan. Listed are tasks such as defining physical site characteristics and design steps such as concept, drawings and plant selection. These steps, when itemized, are understandable and have perceived value to most clients. Add to this an itemized list of site environmental factors to be analyzed, which are less obvious requirements, and client resistance to design fees is broken down even further. A typical itemized design agreement is shown in Figure 12-1.

The Plant Health Care approach can be used to show the value of the design process — that in addition to creating a design, the company will also be collecting samples and will have conducted a detailed environmental analysis of the property.

Plant Health Care can also become a valuable tool to sell the installation of the completed landscape plan. Many clients identify low maintenance as one of the most desirable characteristics of a landscape. Clients should be shown how plants were selected for various locations in the landscape and how this attention to ecological requirements of each plant will result in low maintenance. Instilling confidence in the design and installation can play an important role in a landscape warranty, often referred to as a landscape guarantee.

Plant Health Care can also be incorporated into a landscape warranty. Many landscape design/build companies offer a one year "guarantee" on the landscapes they install. Generally the company warrants to replace — one time — any plant that dies within one year of installation. A few companies restrict this replacement period to six months or one growing season and some provide only a free replacement of the plant and charge for installation labor. However, this policy of replacing dead or dying plants does not necessarily lead to client satisfaction. Clients can be pleased that the company stands behind their installation and replaces the plant, but they still had to notify the company that a plant failed and wait for the replacement. A far better approach would be a situation where the client does not need to inspect the landscape. This is the basis of the PHC approach to a landscape installation warranty. Many clients are aware of the concept of extended warranties. It is a common purchase option for many products from electrical appliances to cars. Plant Health Care can be used as part of an extended warranty for the landscape. Rather than offering a guarantee, the PHC warranty provides protection from plant losses and more importantly, ensures a quality appearance of the landscape. The PHC warranty not only provides for the one-time replacement of any plant that dies,

> *Plant Health Care can become a valuable tool to sell the installation of the completed landscape plan.*

> *PHC can be used as part of an extended warranty...*

Landscape Company Name

DESIGN AGREEMENT

Client name _____

Address _____

The following services will be performed to prepare the landscape plan for the _____
_____ landscape at _____.

SITE ANALYSIS

Environmental analysis of the site

_____ Soil pH

_____ Soil fertility

_____ Soil profile analysis

_____ Soil texture

_____ Soil drainage

_____ Soil compaction

_____ Define site micro-climates

_____ Determine exposures

Defining the physical characteristics of the site

_____ Property and structure measurements

_____ Checking utility locations

_____ Defining views

DESIGN

_____ Concepts

_____ Scale drawing

_____ Selection of plant materials that match design needs and environmental conditions

The design fee for this project is $_____.

All design fees will be credited to the account at the time of billing for the landscape installation.

Client's Signature _____ / Date _____

Designer's Signature _____ / Date _____

Figure 12 - 1. Typical content of a design agreement.